THE BOOK OF UNVEILING

FROM AWAKENING TO ABIDANCE

BY

FRED DAVIS

EDITED BY JOHN AMES

The Book of Unveiling
From Awakening to Abidance
© 2015 Fred Davis

Published in the US by Awakening Clarity Press

ISBN 13: 978-1-5148-4602-5
ISBN 10: 1-5148-4602-0

Edited by John Ames
Cover design and interior design by www.jimandzetta.com

THIS BOOK IS DEDICATED TO
MY CLIENTS AND STUDENTS
ALL AROUND THE WORLD.

THANK YOU.

ACKNOWLEDGEMENTS

MY HEARTFELT THANKS AND LOVE TO MY FAMILY

BETSY

WILLY

JACK

&

DICKENS

WHO HAVE TAUGHT ME MUCH
ABOUT LIFE AND LOVE
AND ENLIGHTENMENT—
AND HOW TO DREAM LIKE A KING.

ALL OF THE ARTICLES IN THIS BOOK
ORGINALLY APPEARED AS POSTS ON
AWAKENINGCLARITYNOW.COM, FRED'S WEBSITE,
WHICH HAS HUNDREDS OF PAGES OF VALUABLE
RESOURCES FOR BOTH SEEKERS AND FINDERS.

OTHER BOOKS BY FRED DAVIS

THE BOOK OF UNDOING
DIRECT POINTING TO NONDUAL AWARENESS

THE BOOK OF UNKNOWING
FROM ENLIGHTENMENT TO EMBODIMENT

BEYOND RECOVERY
NONDUALITY AND THE TWELVE STEPS

TABLE OF CONTENTS

"We don't suffer from
what we *think,*
we suffer from
what we *believe.*"

~Fred Davis

WHAT AWAKENING IS—AND ISN'T!

I recently got an interesting email from an ex-client of mine. This is someone who could hear me very clearly—until he woke up! At that point, as often happens, he was then content to fly by his own guidance again, which told him something along the lines of "You finally got this thing! You did it! This is all there is, too! When you got it, you got it ALL!!"

This reaction is very common. It happened to me. When I woke up I just KNEW that no one had ever gone THERE before. And wasn't I special? That notion was a combination of innocence and hubris, and it was off, but only by about a mile. So it happens, and it happens a lot.

The only thing that makes this particular guy stand out is that he did the same thing time after time without learning anything, which is the definition of an addict. This guy was an addict for the thrill of freshly awakening. It's a powerful drug, but the problem with the awakening addiction is that in order to feed it, you have to repeatedly pretend to go back to sleep.

Finally we quit working together, but not before I told this young man what I've told lots and lots of clients, readers, and other seekers.

1. Awakening is typically an event-style recognition that doesn't happen to anyone; it only happens to Awakeness itself.
2. There is a spiritual experience that accompanies many awakenings. That spiritual experience is simply a flashy vehicle that's carrying a brown paper package. All the stuff that counts is in the package, but we typically get fixated on the vehicle. We share our experiences, and then other people get fixated on these vehicles before they even have

13

    one, and that fixation may keep them from ever receiving the brown paper package.

3. For almost everyone, and I personally know of no exception, awakening is a vertical arising on a horizontal line. We clear, we wake up, and we clear some more, hopefully a lot more, as we move in the direction of abidance and embodiment. We do not get to graduate like we do in high school, nor do we get to pass Go and collect $200 like we do in Monopoly. The balance of our clearing is gradual, though it may be sparked quite often with new insights that can feel like new awakenings. In between those insights we may experience what we call oscillation, which is simply consciousness re-identifying with the unit.

4. You are beyond space and time, but that unit you're wearing lives right slap dab in the middle of both. Thus, on the illusory relative level, it will appear to take time for clearing to occur. It may take years. Conscious Awakeness has been flowing through the Fred unit for more than eight years, and trust me, it is not up for graduation.

5. Continued clearing means continued attention on clearing. This calls for consistent—not just episodic—patience, humility, and work. If you don't have a lot more of those things than I did, then settle down and plan to stay at it for quite a while.

Given our history, I can't know if my ex-client still feels today like he did a few days ago when he had this latest realization, but the truth is here in this email, regardless of who is, or is not, currently seeing it, so I present it to you.

> *Hey Fred,*
>
> *So I came across this quote from Adyashanti and it really hit me, and really humbled me. I wanted to see if you can confirm that this is indeed what you have been telling me all along regarding working towards embodiment....*
>
> *He says, "The enlightenment I speak of is not simply a realization, not simply the discovery of one's true nature. That discovery is just the beginning—the point of entry into an inner revolution. This realization of one's true nature does not guarantee this revolution; it simply makes it possible."*

He goes on to say, "This revolution is a breaking away from the old, repetitive, dead structures of thought and perception that humanity finds itself trapped in. Realization of the ultimate Reality is a direct and sudden existential awakening to one's true nature that opens the door to the possibility of an inner revolution. Such a revolution requires an ongoing emptying out of the old structures of consciousness and the birth of a living and fluid intelligence."

So what you refer to as clearing up, he refers to in this as an inner revolution. But you guys are saying the same thing, yes?

I can't tell you how humbling it is to recognize this. You've called me a baby throwing a temper tantrum in the past, demanding my enlightenment to appear now and suddenly and permanently, and I understood it at the time, but now it has really sunk in and I fully appreciate the fault in the position I've been taking.

I'm shocked by my arrogance up until now... This realigns things on a whole new path, with a whole new attitude... One you've been urging me, not so subtly, towards for some time now. I have sure been one stubborn, immature, arrogant human...

This is a lesson that many of us have to learn and relearn. Me included.

DEAR SEEKER

Dear Seeker,

Before I officially launch into the true body of this letter, let me first unofficially point out the obvious, because I've noticed that it's the obvious stuff that spiritual folks seem to miss most often. Hide in plain sight, I always say.

It's no accident that you're reading this, and the timing has not come about by chance. There is no such thing as an accident, not anything called "chance," and no alternative to What Is. Seems like there might be, seems like there should be. Isn't.

This is it. This is It.

What I mean is that outside of a maniac's mind—of which there are roughly 7,000,000,000 on just this planet—there simply is no such thing as "what isn't." You probably find that disappointing, given that you've tried to spend the great bulk of your life there. Do you notice that you've always failed?

In the end, it's always back to This, from which you never left. Funny thing, reality.

Where was I? Oh, I was saying that there is no "what isn't." Seems awfully blunt, does it not? One has to ask if that notion might be introduced with just a little hedge. Just the tiniest hedge would be oh-so-much-more comfortable and comforting.

The answer is No. There is no shoulda-coulda-woulda. No mistakes, no accidents, no chance, no alternatives. Ever. Not anytime, not anywhere, not in any form whatsoever, and there are no exceptions to the Universal Law of It Is What It Is. So your mind can just throw in the towel and quit looking for them. Won't that be a rest!

I don't want to make it sound like everything is cast in stone ahead of time. It's not. If you want to name the apparent methodology of This Happening, then name it "Spontaneous Fate." Don't you love that? Now there's a phrase that says something!

For the moment, forget what you think you know, and listen to Me. And oh, pardon me, I "should" have introduced Myself earlier, except that there's no place for "should" in reality. Reality is. I am.

I am This. I am This Itself. Hi to me the reader over there, too, which is not other than this very This that I am. I am this arising. This arising is how This Happening is showing up just now. To itself.

And what is This? Excellent question, and like most excellent questions, there are many excellent answers. It depends on who you ask.

For the witness, there is just This Happening. Only. And This Happening is not actually other than That which witnesses it, although it can seem like it is. Seems so. Isn't. There's a lot of that sort of thing going on in This Happening, and there's nothing happening outside of This Happening, because there is no "outside" of This Happening.

Oneness is Oneness or it's not. And if Oneness is indeed Oneness, then everything has to be included in Oneness. Makes sense, does it not? By this I mean that relativity is not excluded. No matter the ultimate "real or unreal" nature of relativity, it is My Experience, it is This Happening, and it absolutely counts.

Speaking of Oneness, what is it that you are, Dear Reader? The cat's coming out of the bag!

You are part of This Happening. Not a "separate" part, because there is no separation anywhere, neither in space nor time, given that you made both of them up to begin with. But you are welcome to appear separate if it suits your fancy. It's a popular fashion statement, which is fine. Unity welcomes diversity and multiplicity, and then calls itself unicity. How sweet.

A rose is a rose is a rose, Gertrude Stein told us, and she was right, too!

And where are you, Dear Reader? Clearly I can see that you are Here. Surely you have to confess that yourself—there's no getting out of it. Where would you go, when you're All That Is, As It Is?

You can't be somewhere else, because there is no "somewhere else." The land of "somewhere else" would have to border the land of "what isn't," which is a slippery way to say that it exists only in the imagination of crazy people. Of which there is no lack.

But if you go to New York today you'll be Here when you get there, and wherever you left from, although you'll now tag it "there," will actually only exist in—three guesses—your imagination. First guess, good job!

When are you, Dear Reader? You are Now. You are the Now, this Now, the only Now. You are the Now, and the Now, and the Now. There is only Now. There's no past, no future, no what isn't, no somewhere else. You are Here Now.

To be clear, I don't mean that you are present in some Here and Now, especially not some other Here and Now. Heaven forbid. I am stating as plainly as I can state that your Presence is the Here and Now. Right here, right now!

But let's not get hung up on the Absolute. After all that's only a view. The Absolute view shows beyond the shadow of a doubt that the Absolute is all there is. Except when it's not. After all, what is the sky without stars? What is the ocean without waves?

How about the relative view, my Dear Witness? You can't rule out what you've already ruled in. After all, those are the rules, and they're your rules.

It's just like your unit going along with What Is. What choice does it actually have? There's no point in resisting what you have already accepted. It's already a done deal; clearly there's no point in fighting what's already Here. How much do you want to suffer? That's the only question.

Now, I'm not saying that relativity does or does not ultimately matter, but I am saying that it counts. If you try to override your experience with highfalutin philosophy then you are woefully lost in the dream. Deal with relativity as if it matters: you can't go wrong doing that. And, ultimately, that's what happens anyway. In the end, claw marks or no claw marks, action happens.

The content of This Happening continuously changes, but This Itself never does. I am not still, I am Stillness. I am That Which Does Not Move. It is from This Itself that This Happening is born, although some wise folk might reasonably argue with that "born" term.

Appears! There we have it! It is from This Itself that This Happening appears. Continually, without beginning, without end, rebirthing and reinventing itself every moment of every millennium.

And you are This Itself. You can't not be! Oneness is Oneness or it's not, right?

I am This Itself, too. We are One, but we are not the same. We are talking about Oneness, not sameness. What a bore sameness would be. Heck, you've got that when you're playing Void!

I experience myself as This Happening. You experience yourself as This Happening. And we can't say that This Happening is other than me, you, us. It's not like anyone has a lock on the market.

So is there any difference in this One Thing that is showing up as the two things—you and I, between these not-two intersections of Indra's Net? Oddly enough, yes! Well, yes and no. There's a lot of that here, too.

I, the animating presence that is within, without, and throughout the typist, a.k.a. the Fred unit, know I am This. It is not just in my thinking, it is in my experience, and more and more it is in my living. Given that I am Life Itself, that progression just makes sense, does it not?

Other than that, there's no other real difference between the Reader and the Writer, except for the fact that that Knowing makes all the difference. Hope this helped.

Love,

Your Self

DO WE CREATE OUR OWN REALITY?

I recently answered a couple of email questions for a client that I think warrant being publicly aired. Here are both his questions and my answers.

Question

> *"Hi, Fred. I wonder what your take is on the notion that we "create our reality" with our thoughts and feelings. Of course I'm talking about the relative plane, since I understand that Reality is the eternal field that is not created or creatable. Do you have a sense that what shows up in our experience is moldable by the influence of our thinking and feelings or would you put outcomes and circumstances as beyond any control within our ability to influence or manipulate?"*

Answer

Hi, Larry. This is a well-asked question, especially since you're indicating two views. In this case, there are actually three: relative, universal, and nondual. A great deal of nondual spirituality/ philosophy is taught from the universal view rather than the nondual, and this complicates an already difficult teaching.

This answer is being written for you, though I may use it for an article later. Every unit always thinks the satsang teacher or the spiritual writer is addressing everyone at once, when in truth the teacher or writer is always addressing whoever has posed the question. We can effectively gather general information from what is said to an apparent individual, but through such gathering misunderstandings may arise.

So be clear that this answer is being written specifically for you—for what appears as and is commonly known as the Larry unit. Of course what's actually happening is that Oneness is speaking directly to Oneness through both the Fred and Larry units. On we go.

The following synopsis is necessarily simplistic in the cause of brevity. For that same reason it does not attempt to be "nondually correct."

Three Views

Relative teachings masquerading as "true" teachings are those which are taught in opposition to teaching that isn't derived from a particular tribe and tradition. "We're right and you're wrong, regardless of what you're teaching." From the relative view "X" is true.

Universal teachings masquerading as "nondual" teachings are those which are taught in opposition to our "normal" relative understanding. From the universal view, "Z" is true. We've moved to the other side of the equation, but "We're still right and you're still wrong."

However, from the nondual view, "Y" is true, and for our purposes here we'll regard "Y" as standing for both "X" and "Z" being simultaneously true.

In other words, "We're all right."

The nondual view makes the mind extremely uncomfortable; however, every large spiritual insight I've ever had has always pointed to a "both/and" answer, never to an "either/or." First I see that the opposite of how I had things figured out is true, and then, later perhaps, I'll see that the full view contains both.

The mind is a relative, either/or mechanism, just like a computer, which is why we interface so well with computers. Mind and computer both ask "Is the switch off or on?"; "Is the answer 0 or 1?"; "Is it less than 45 or more than 45?".

Everyone starts their spiritual story from the same place: the relative plane. We start out believing in, and acting from, one half of the yin-yang: "I am Fred; I am the body." We are living in 180 degrees of the truth. It's true as far as it goes, but it doesn't go far enough.

Upon awakening and having our first look from the universal view, we typically jump straight to the other half of the yin-yang. "I am Not-Fred; I am the Vastness." We are living in the other 180 degrees of the truth. It's true as far as it goes, but it doesn't go far enough.

Mind now has choices, and it wants to know, which is the right one? Am I the little man or the Vastness? Both. This last understanding, that you are Oneness that includes both the little man and the Vastness is what's missed in a lot of teachings.

So, with that covered let's address your question on manifestation.

Larry, once we see for ourselves that this whole thing, inclusive of the unit we thought we were, is a dream, we immediately recognize that anything can happen anywhere at any time. So, is it possible that in the dream we can influence events and outcomes?

It may appear so, within the confines of the dream. There are a couple of things to note. The one who's trying to manifest, typically for its own benefit, is a dream character, so none of this manifesting is authentic spirituality, it's dream management. It's just a dream character trying out the mechanics of the dream. If it appears that its own behavior brought about a desirable end in the dream for a dream character, then it will probably repeat that behavior—within the dream.

In truth, there is no separation or division of any kind. Everything is happening at the same time. There is no direct cause and effect. Everything is the cause —and the effect—of everything else. There is just one thing going on.

I used to work with manifesting stuff maybe 35 years ago. It wasn't at all mainstream back then. Let me tell you what my issue is with such activity. We start out with a lie. See, I don't actually know what's good for my character, and I don't have the slightest clue about what's good for the Whole. Everything is tied to everything else, so even if my character ends up appearing to manifest what it wanted, if it's not in alignment with everything else, the result may not be a good thing.

It really is the old "be careful what you ask for."

Now, let me go a little further. What actually changes your world is your view. When you change where you're looking from, what you're looking at changes.

If you look at the world *as* the Larry unit, you are going to find problems and suffering. You can't not: it's built in. It's the relative view.

If you look at world *through* the Larry unit, if you use it as the camera that it is instead of as the photographer that it always thought it was, then you'll see one, single, perfect field where everything is simply happening, and it's happening beyond any beliefs, opinions, or positions that various units may have about it.

The Book of Unveiling – From Awakening to Abidance

This is the universal view. I AM. It Is what It Is. And there is no alternative.

The nondual view would be that yes, everything is absolutely perfect! AND I'm just going to tweak this thing over here, or say that to that person over there, or pick something up, or put something down—take some kind of action—to see if I can, paradoxically, make it "more perfect later." Makes no sense. Doesn't have to. Welcome to true, full, nondual spirituality.

Question

> *"Second question has to do with what you recommend in dealing with difficult emotions, such as fear, guilt, shame, etc. Most nondual teachings encourage a non-resistant embracing of such feelings as they arise, and/or a curiosity of what they are made of or the examining of the self that identifies with them. It feels like, though I've glimpsed this awakened state I still find a strong return to separation when these feelings arise in me."*

Answer

First thing, whose fear, guilt, and shame are we talking about? Larry's. Have we ever found a Larry? No. We looked long and hard, and we could not find a Larry. Finally we concluded that there is no Larry. So your question is not really about feelings and emotions, it's about identification. And this, of course, is the foundation of the dream.

Ego wants to tell us that the content of the present arising as well as the answer to our questions are really important, even vital. I fully sympathize with this position, but it's not a true one. All that really matters is who is experiencing the present arising and who is asking the question. If you actually turn you attention around and look, can you find the experiencer? No.

This use of your attention to investigate what's true is vital. I call it "hitting the wall." Investigate your thoughts. Suffering arises when we take our thoughts seriously. This is the truth.

You write, "It feels like, though I've glimpsed this awakened state I still find a strong return to separation when these feelings arise in me," but can you locate this "I..me" you're speaking of? No. Can you find the one who glimpsed reality? No. Be careful though. Just reminding yourself of this won't help you nearly so much as looking and finding the negative answer. Hit the wall.

 23

The "I" that is reading these words is the eternal "I." The ordinary consciousness that's taking this in is the Tao, God, Awareness, Brahman, or what have you that is confused and thinks it's a Larry. What's really going on here is that Oneness is writing to Oneness with the suggestion that the point of light notice that it's not just a point of light (or Larryness), but that it's the Whole Thing. Here is a short exercise you might find helpful in eliminating the side-effects of this kind of misidentification.

Sit in a chair. Relax as best you can, but an alert posture is helpful. Now close your eyes and let a feeling that causes separation arise in you, fear for example. Let it take you. Let it do its worst. Don't fight it.

Notice that you don't actually die. Notice that you could handle the fear indefinitely if you had to. My guess is that you'll see it spike up and then wind down, because without resistance it will simply pass through the body. It may very well go away. If and when it begins to arise, repeat the process. Allow it to come and allow it to go.

Eventually, you might come to a point where you can welcome it, because suffering is the alarm clock in the dream. It's telling you that you are in misidentification. Inquire, investigate, allow. What can fear, guilt, or shame actually do to you, except point the way home?

MUCH ADO ABOUT NOTHING

As many of you already know from your own so-called "personal experience," there is no "personal you" present inside the unit that's reading this line. Given that you either know this from your own experience or that you've heard it and read it time and again from what you probably consider to be reasonably reliable sources, it might be worth your while to try doing that thing you are told to "never do" in nondual spirituality. Why not pretend that it's true, at least long enough to ask yourself the following questions: "Hmmm... If there's no "me" actually here, how in the world am 'I' going to wake up? Who is going to wake up if 'I' do?"

Oops. Have you possibly missed something in the logic loop? I did, and I missed it for a long time. Let's look at it.

Who is it that's hoping to wake up? Do you actually know? You might want to find out who it is that's been trying and failing to achieve enlightenment, whether it's an initial awakening or a fresh shot of truth to fan the flames of that stale old experience you had weeks, or months, or years ago but which you still love to think about and talk about to anyone who'll listen. (I did that too, by the way.) You know that something profound happened and you know that you learned something really important, but you can no longer quite remember just what that important thing was that you've now forgotten.

It's terribly frustrating, is it not? The agony of NO taste of truth can only be surpassed by the agony of NO MORE taste of truth. What I like to say in these instances, or in a similar instance where we report that we "know all this stuff intellectually," is that when we come to clarity we instantly see that the only thing we were previously missing was the only thing that counts. Enlightenment is all about right now. Only. Ever.

In my case, whatever it is that I Am was breathlessly waiting for Fred to wake up for years—10 long winters and summers of them before I got a break. I'm speaking of my first big glimpse, in 1992. It was short but deep and of course incredibly sweet. It would be another 14 years of breathless waiting before it happened again. Oddly, what might be thought of as the biggest disappointment of all is that Fred never did wake up. Not in 1992 and not in 2006. I woke up, mind you, but Fred didn't.

I remember one time years ago when I was sitting down to host a little satsang inside a local health food store. This was prior to my discovering I was going to end up with a near-zero local audience for this teaching that I was so sure everyone was hot to hear about. After all, I thought, who didn't want to live FREE? Pretty much everybody, it turned out. Which works out really nicely since nearly everyone will, in fact, end their lives in the very same condition they started them in, by which I mean deep sleep.

Anyway, I was trying to make an introductory point to the one guy at the table whom I knew hardly at all. I'm not claiming it was skillful, but I said, "Larry, if I ever tell you I'm enlightened, run."

"Don't worry, I will!" he promised.

"But if I tell you that I'm not enlightened, I'm lying there as well." I thought it was a pretty cool opener.

I can see now that it wasn't a skillful way to open a meeting—perhaps I was just trying to be mystical and mysterious. Though I misfired, I was attempting to make the no-Fred point, and the guy at whom I had aimed the comment had completely missed the point. He never came back to another satsang, and come to think of it, the first one was so bad that we never had a second meeting! My point is that this you-no-you, Fred-no-Fred thing can be slippery.

It's been proven historically that the easiest way to find out what you are is by first finding out what you are not. The Hindus call it "neti neti," which means "not this, not that." The Christians call it "via negativa," which is Latin for "the negative way." The discovery of what you are not won't take you all the way home, but it will at least set you up for going home. It'll get you past the sand traps and put you on the green, so to speak, and then all that's left is some highly skilled putting.

To get you familiar with what I'm talking about, let's take a crack at finding whatever it is that I Am not. Let's look for "Fred." Oh, what the hell, let me save you a lot of time and bother. It would be sadistic of me to expect you to go through what I went through in order to find myself blessedly empty-handed. You can't find "Fred" anywhere.

There isn't one. Never has been and never will be. Fred is

nothing more than a projection, a collective agreement, or a common lie, depending on how you want to look at it. We can easily find the tracks of a Fred, but we can never find the thing itself.

Some of you may remember the *Winnie the Pooh* story where Pooh and Piglet go around and around a tree in search of mysterious and furtive Woozles. The number of tracks multiply rapidly and they become more and more concerned until Christopher Robin points out that the tracks are, in fact, their very own. Christopher Robin plays the role of guru in that story, much like I find myself playing the guru in this one. Oh boy.

I remember speaking at a Unity church one night. When I got through, a woman asked me if I thought there was really a mass awakening going on, and if the world was really in trouble. I curved my arm over my head and pointed down at it. "Madam, if this," I said in reference to myself, "if this is at the front of the room talking, believe me the world is in trouble!"

However you choose to look at it, Fred is, in the end, an utter fiction that not only is not, but could not have ever been and cannot ever come to be. Trust me on this; I looked longer and harder than most of you can imagine.

How is it that whatever it is that I Am can calmly sit here and declare that there is no Fred? Try this: Given that there's only One Thing Going On, where is there room for an independent entity? I would rest my case here, but many of you would remain unconvinced.

If I am sitting in my big chair in the living room, and a friend walks into the room, unless he is presently awake, he is going to see what he takes to be his friend Fred. In that case, I imagine that he would smile and say "Hello."

On the other hand, if a burglar, a stranger who was not previously indoctrinated into the Fred myth, came through the same door into the same room, he would not see a Fred. He would likely neither smile nor say "Hello." No. If the Fred unit is lucky, the burglar would say something to the effect of "Holy moley! The owner is home!" and skedaddle at a high rate of speed. If the Fred unit is not so lucky, the burglar might hit it in the head with a large hammer and then go about trying to find something worth stealing and turning a handsome profit on. Good luck with that, Stranger-Who-Is-My-Own-Self.

Whatever it is that I Am, I know that there is no Fred with absolutely brilliant clarity and unflinching sureness, but that does not preclude a sense of Fredness, a sense which is being experienced by Awakeness through an apparently operational (and totally lunatic) independent entity. When I say "Awakeness" I refer to the Indescribable Mystery Which I Am that is called by numerous names.

You are welcome to call me Tao or Consciousness, Brahman or Awareness, Oneness, or even God— whatever floats your boat. It's also okay to simply call me Fred if you're referring to this apparent typist. There's no point in giving the unit something to take on airs about. However, if you wish to be more exacting in your language, then "Fredness" would be more accurate.

Imagine that a suit of clothes was somehow walking across your yard. You could name it anything you wanted, but it would still be an empty suit of clothes, however animated and magicked-up it might be. If you take a close look at Fredness you'll notice that the lights are on, but there's nobody at home. It's a reserved coach for Awakeness, a vehicle always at the ready to continue going nowhere while appearing to go somewhere. It's quite a trick.

Now, just to put a finer point on it, Fredness refers to a series of patterns, many of which are discernible—even at a distance—to other units who think of themselves as being human bodies and thus assume this unit is one as well. "Oh, what a tangled web we weave, when first we practice to deceive." They are deeply confused units. Just as You are if You think You are limited to being a single human body. Ridiculous!

Granted, this unit walks, talks, acts, and appears to think in an identifiable repetitive manner. Thus the confused units will say, "Oh, look, there's Fred." But since there is no Fred here—or anywhere else—what they mean is "Oh, look, there's Fredness."

Still, whatever it is that I Am, I certainly have a sense of Fred. That sense was here prior to Awakening's taking on a conscious role through this unit, and it's still here in post-awakening. It will be here so long as there is a body; it's just a matter of degree. Christ and Buddha had it. I have it, you've got it. It's a universal malady. And even though you are doing as I advised in the beginning of this piece and are considering the possibility that there is no individual you, there is still the relative world to be contended with. It doesn't disappear, however "far" you have come.

Jesus would have turned around to answer if St. Paul had come up behind him and said, "Hey, Jesus, what's up?"; however, he would not have done so because he thought he was confined to being a single human being. He would have turned because it was the practical thing to do in the relative world. Awakeness was finding Itself experiencing through the Jesus unit. Without Jesus having at least some subtle identification, the unit's biology would wither and die, which would mark the end of the Jesus story.

Jesus referenced this point with his "Render unto Caesar what is Caesar's" remark about taxes, and we can likewise say, "When in Rome, do as the Romans do." Why not? I can pretend that I've completely transcended Rome, but if I do it's a sure sign that I'm up to my butt in it. Not answering to your name is not a sign that you are awake. Denying the value and everyday relevance of the relative world is denying a big part of nondual spirituality, so denying is neither enlightened nor helpful.

I recently read a fairly detailed review of my work that was generally quite positive, and I'm certainly not sorry it was published. However, the reviewer deducted "Enlightenment Points," whatever those are, because I give a damn about the relative you and about our planet. I plead guilty to those charges, and let the "Enlightenment Points" fall where they may. There's no one here to care.

PICKING AN ARGUMENT WITH REALITY

This cloudiness problem, as you may have already guessed (or hoped), is a "unit thing." Isn't it great to have a unit to blame all of our unconsciousness on? We love to think of ourselves as being sort of like glorified mail carriers, relentless Seekers of Truth who will be deterred by "neither snow nor rain nor heat nor gloom of night." It's lovely, but is it even close to being realistic?

I would guess that the Number One Comment that comes up in Clarity Sessions runs something like this: "I was doing great, and then..." I could fill in the rest of that sentence with a universal truth that states, "and then I picked an argument with Reality." It's not just true some of the time, it's true all of the time, every time.

Now, let's be clear. You—meaning You with a capital "Y"—are beyond space and time. Space and time both appear within You. But how about that unit? Oh. It lives smack-dab in the middle of both. And "there's the rub," as Shakespeare's Hamlet told us.

You with a capital "Y" are all-accepting; indeed, You are Acceptance itself. But that unit? Not so much.

I've named the unit that's typing this column "Mr. Resistance," whom I envision as being sort of like Mr. Clean, except my version is short the earring, big muscles, and smile, and is only bald on the back of its head. Yes, I with a capital "I" laugh and smile a lot on the outside, but this unit holds a resentment against... well...everything. Mr. Resistance is opposed to Reality. All of it.

That's the way of units. They don't give a damn what God is up to with all his big-picture, big-shot plans—it's all about them. Interestingly, it's all about every one of them. Notice how your vision works. It places that unit in the center of the universe no matter where it looks. Isn't it lovely to discover that apparently it really is "all about you?"

Sound works much the same way. Mr. Resistance doesn't know or care how anyone else hears anything when all sounds are clearly coming straight to the center of his ear, which of course is the only important ear in the universe. None of those other ears have a license or even his permission to listen in on his world. They are outlaws, he is king. And so it goes.

There are 7,000,000,000 centers of the universe on this planet alone. No wonder we have so much conflict! No wonder we're tearing the planet to pieces. There simply isn't enough to go around—for them. Mr. Resistance is barely making do with the whole thing; there's no way (or reason) for him to share any of it. Such an idea!

Because these units live in space and time, it takes time for Awakeness to colonize the unit. The unit never actually wakes up—it doesn't have the capacity to wake up—but the zillions of unskillful patterns it's composed of are eventually—very very slowly in my case— replaced by more skillful ones. If the unit lives long enough, remains open, stays alert, and pays careful attention, then it can eventually (I am told) fully embody That Which Is Beyond the Dream and do so within the dream. So living long enough, remaining open, staying alert, and paying careful attention is our job, which leads to the dream becoming more and more conscious.

Which apparently is the "goal-less goal," although I confess that God is not actually confiding all of Her secrets to me. (Even though She should.)

Now, no one forces you to do your job. You are welcome to hold out as long as you want. There's not even a penalty for your doing so if you can overlook the suffering that living unconsciously causes. And God forbid you should choose to live unconsciously after you first wake up. It can certainly be done—I did it!—but you will learn what the words "agonizing torment" mean.

You might as well go ahead and get over the New Year's resolution thing. There's no point in telling yourself, "Okay, I get it, and by golly I'm going to surrender to all arisings from here on out." It's nice to say, and nice for your ear to hear, but you ain't gonna do it because you're not actually in control of that unit. Oops.

What you are in control of is where you place your attention. If, after you wake up, you will simply devote yourself to witnessing that unit's unskillful patterns right now, then you've done all you can do, and all that you need to do. Once there's enough clarity to truly see that those patterns no longer serve you, that they are not beneficial, then they'll naturally drop away as part of the unit's evolutionary process.

The unit can't fix the unit, just as the voice in your head can't fix the voice in your head. Be the nonjudgmental witness. That's all that's required. Just notice what that unit does, what it thinks, what it feels. Play Spot-the-Unskillful-Pattern with yourself. Any other activity or judgment you take up is just ego building itself up while appearing to tear itself down.

Mr. Resistance is going to hate Me for sharing this. To heck with him. Good luck anyway.

A FUNNY THING HAPPENED ON THE WAY TO SURRENDER

Some time back, I cut a video called "Surrendering to the Unit." Had I been trying to draw a crowd, I would have labeled it "Conquering the Unit" or "Beating Down the Ego." With a title like that, it would have gotten a whole lot more views than it did. However, since surrender has proven to be such a rewarding lifestyle for me, I went ahead and used the dreaded "S" word anyway. And having used it again in the title of this piece, I realize I have doomed it to being one of the least popular in this book, but sometimes you just have to say what you need to say and popularity be damned.

Yes, I publicly plead guilty to the charge of going along with God. I've found life too painful when I don't. I have concluded that what happens on this planet does not have to have been weighed and calculated in my head first. I was not nearly so flexible for most of my life and I suffered accordingly. Yet even a blind squirrel can find a nut from time to time, and this blind squirrel stumbled upon the luscious nut of surrender quite a few years ago. Ever since I gave God her job back, it has become more and more clear that the universe is apparently on its own path with its own timetable, as incredible as it may seem to a big shot like me. So, I figure I might as well fall in line before I'm forced to fall in line. It's kind of a "You can't fire me, I quit" sort of thing.

My "Surrendering to the Unit" video explored one example of surrender in my life, and I was pleased with it, but the real unexpected payoff came in the wake of the video; however, before I describe the payoff, here's a quick recap of what I explored in that seven-minute talk.

The video focused on my work habits and my attitude toward them. Everyone around me had long been indicating that I'd been working way too much, often 80+ hours a week, and I had reached the same conclusion many times. I know for some of you it's hard to think of spiritual teaching as "work," and yes, it's a great joy and an honor, but it can still—upon reflection—look and feel a whole lot like something that closely resembles work! The point is that everybody including me held the opinion that I was working too much, but every time I decided to cut my hours, especially the number of my energy-draining Awakening Sessions, I noticed that my decision didn't stick. I slid right back into the same work pattern almost immediately.

Since I'd seen this pointless pattern form and reform so many times without change occurring, I decided that apparently I was supposed to be working as much as I was working, so there was no point in bitching and moaning about it. My resistance to Reality As It Is served no useful purpose. I ended up working the same amount anyway, but in addition to the work, I had to suffer with my handy victim story that I "shouldn't be" working so much. So, faced with a unit that wouldn't quit doing what it was doing, I gave up on trying to work less and willingly submitted to working long, late hours for the duration. If IT wanted to work this unit to death and then go get another, well then, damn it...okay. Why suffer when I can cooperate with the inevitable? End of victim story and end of video.

The evening of the same day that I cut that video, I discovered that I was sitting in my favorite chair in the living room reading a book, something I used to do one or more times a day, every day, without fail, yet this was the first time I had done so in several weeks. I was mightily surprised, but my surprise quickly gave way to delight. Otherwise, I didn't pay much attention to it.

The following morning I found myself in the very same chair, and once again I was reading for pleasure and insight, rather than corresponding with clients on my iPhone or iPad, which is all I had been doing lately in that chair. I really began to wonder what on earth was going on. By that evening, when I once again found myself downstairs with a book in my hand and a cat on the arm of my chair, I knew what was going on because I hadn't ended up there unconsciously. On the way to the chair, a blind pattern had been seen, seen through, penetrated, and was dropping away.

Here's how that happened. When I first thought about going downstairs, I suddenly remembered something I "needed" to do at the computer. I was right at the head of the stairs, and I had to make a decision—would I stay upstairs and work, or go down and read? I strongly considered first going into the study and doing the little chore and then going downstairs to read later. That was the lie I had to see through. I realized that once I'd told that lie and believed it, I could kiss going downstairs goodbye. So I went downstairs and did my reading. Whatever that thing I thought I needed to do was, I notice it kept.

Over the next few days I noticed other lies (patterns within the pattern) as the whole victim story fell apart. I found out that there were Four Big Lies.

First on the list is the lie I saw through at the top of the stairs: "I'll do this first and then I'll take a break." Is it true? No. There is always something additional to do.

Second, "This is really important." Is it true? Rarely. As a matter of fact, my feeling is that most of the time if something really is important, then the "This is really important" thought will not even arise. There'll be no calculation or mental debate: a truly important thing just automatically gets handled.

Third, "I need to do this now." Is it true? Rarely. A session is something I need to show up for right on time, which I generally do. My credo is that "I'm rarely late, but never early." Other than a session, almost anything on my to-do list can wait at least a little while, even until the next day. Noticing this lie keeps me from burning so much midnight oil.

Fourth, "I'm going to do this work now so that I won't be swamped tomorrow." Is it true? No. Because come the morrow, I'll be doing the next day's work, and on and on, so that the cycle never ends.

The following is my process for working with Blind Patterns. It begins with a first step that is really an act of grace or good fortune occurring spontaneously via deepening clarity, and it ends with a fourth step that is virtually automatic if the first three steps have been gone through honestly.

> **SEE IT:** Consciously notice the unit is running an unconscious pattern.
> **SEE THROUGH IT:** Acknowledge the pattern's unskillfulness. The deeper you go the better, and don't deny what you find.
> **BE WILLING:** Accept the possibility that you can be other than the way you are: this is the biggest part of your job.
> **PENETRATE IT:** See it so completely that it begins to drop away by degrees or falls apart altogether.

I went through this process with each of the Four Big Lies individually. The grace, so to speak, was to be able to intuitively sense the movement of an unskillful pattern working through the unit so that I could become conscious enough to watch it work. That's what happened at the top of the stairs.

Some of you are no doubt wondering who the "I" was that eventually gave up its struggle: it was nobody. Struggling simply ceased. In order to talk about it, however, we could say that it was one impersonal metapattern (Fredness) surrendering to another metapattern (apparent manifestation). Fredness permeates this unit through and through in much the same way that the Sense of Being permeates universes and dimensions. As long as Fred's around, he can't be ignored.

I'm still working a lot. That's fine. I love my work. I love talking to clients and volunteers, getting a new post or video put up, tweaking the website, answering mail when I can, and doing the other thousand things it takes to make this teaching run smoothly on a large scale. I'm thinking 60 hours should do it. I'm not watching my watch, but I am watching my lies.

ALIGNING OURSELVES WITH TRUTH

Living Method Awakening Sessions, whether one-on-one or in a group workshop, are nothing like what is typically called satsang. They are not a forum for Q&A or open discussion. They are highly structured and methodical, with a well-defined beginning, middle, and end. The client never knows where we are—don't need to—but I always do. I often have to squelch someone's ego, sometimes fairly forcefully, in order to establish the proper climate where Truth will most naturally become apparent.

Egos don't mean any harm; they're just used to being heard and are always hoping to have their way. And of course they are self-referencing authorities on every topic known to man. They are always vying for attention and craving control. Our egos generally don't like being told that we are passengers in any situation; we prefer to be—at the very least—copilots. I get it. I'm a human being, too, and I can be as guilty as anyone else.

Thus, one of the most important parts of my job, so to speak, is to take the wheel from these co-pilots and escort them to the passenger compartment. It's absolutely critical that I get clients in alignment with me, and by extension with the Truth they say they seek. In every Awakening Session we get to find out if they really want the truth.

Everyone takes their views so seriously. We are the Important Ones, and by God we are the Right Ones! Getting help in recognizing the folly of this whole line of thinking is the very thing we come to a teacher for, but often we recognize our folly only in hindsight. The good news is that most people whose egos I've had to realign have woken up shortly thereafter, and suddenly those egoic grudges just disappear—poof!

If we are going to wake up by any means short of a spontaneous shot of grace that totally overpowers us, then we are going to have to be willing to unlearn a great deal of what we think we know. I like to point out that there are good reasons why *The Book of Undoing* is not titled *Let's Just Do This One More Thing* and why *The Book of Unknowing* is not titled *The Book of Let's Just Get a Little More Information.*

Sometimes in a session someone will make a blanket statement about something they "know they know," and I'll ask, "Are you willing unknow that?" These are the times when it becomes clear who is willing to be set free on Awakeness' terms and who wants to be set free on their own terms. No one wakes up on their own terms. Awakeness displays itself how it wants, to whom it wants, when it wants to, and that's that. There's no way that holding back and waking up are ever going to occur at the same time. One negates the other. And a key form of holding back is being unwilling to let go of what you know you know.

I spent this past weekend in Asheville, North Carolina at an Awakening Workshop. It was very successful. Anyone who showed up to that meeting who was not consciously awake when they got there, was consciously awake when they left. As usual, there were a couple of people that I had to help get aligned with me, but in the end we got there. We all went to dinner together afterward, and everyone seemed quite happy.

But what if there's no one to help us with alignment? What if we're going into an important session with our teacher, and we're not sure that we're "quite there yet"? Or perhaps we're going into a retreat. People can walk into the greatest retreat in the world and walk out unchanged if there is not a willingness to be other than the way they are. The examples of divine spirit overriding human determination are too rare to even bother talking about. So, as the song asks, "What's a girl to do?"

We provide our own alignment, that's what we do. Alignment with Truth is inevitably the call for surrender. In my sessions, I suggest surrender, and if it's not forthcoming, then I will essentially force the issue. The client "gives," or there is nowhere to go. I remember a couple of years ago I was talking to a woman from Australia who had come to believe a bit of nonsense—I have no recollection of what it was.

I suggested she "give" in her own best interest, and she refused. I pushed, and she still refused to let go. She wanted to share her view with me, and she was rather incredulous that I didn't share the same view. Clients tend to forget who paid whom, and why. So, in order to help her, I forced it, and her ego still would not back down.

This person was more interested in being right than she was in being free. That's actually quite common in our community, although few such people come to me. This teaching exists because there are people who are ready for it. Can't not be; it's two ends of the same stick. It's hard to give up being right, and the client in Australia got to be right. Once I saw that we no longer had a common goal, I stopped the session. She went her way and I went mine. Things are always just as they should be, and this was no exception.

So, precisely how do we provide our own alignment if there's no one around to do it for us? Three words: surrender, surrender, surrender. Don't worry about who's surrendering to what. That above our pay grade; just be willing to do it. And precisely how do we surrender? There is no how-to about it. It just happens.

We already know all we need to know about surrender: we do it twice a day, once when we go to sleep, and again when we wake up. How do we "make" sleeping happen? How do we "make" waking up happen? We don't. Something either stirs or ceases to stir, and we somehow become willing to give up this world for an unknown world, and surrender simply happens. We go to sleep; we wake up. Simple.

How do you put your hair out if it accidentally catches on fire? No one needs to tell you how. You just do it because that's what has to happen. There's not a shred of resistance to having a head that is not on fire. We don't need to think our way through it. The body will take care of it all by itself. If there is any way possible, the fire will be handled. If it's not, we burn. Simple.

We don't do surrender. We become completely willing to be other than the way we are, and then we are surrendered.

Well, damn, look at this. I planned on a short article, and the Universe had other plans. You see who won, don't you? IT always wins. That's why when an hour ago I noticed this might run longer than planned, I just shrugged and kept on writing. I don't want to put my feet down and refuse to be used however IT wants to use me. I've done that before. It ended up ugly. Lesson learned.

In other times, I might have suffered over this change of plan, but I no longer have the capacity for pain that I used to have. These days, if I start to suffer, I will generally see through it almost immediately. I can't overlook suffering any more, because it's so out of tune with the rest of my life. Why do we suffer? It's always the same why: we have misidentified with the unit. As incredible as it may seem, we think we are limited to the unit. Ridiculous, but it's ever so easy to think that. Until it isn't.

Let us have the humility to become other than the way we are. Let us be willing to do it again and again. Let us surrender our selves to our Self. There is no other way for continuous unfolding to happen. There is no other opening for a miracle to occur.

INSTABILITY VERSUS OSCILLATION

For a long time I thought there were two states immediately available in post-awakening: oscillation and stability. That's not true. There's another available state that has been staring me in the face for two years—I just never recognized it. As those of you who have woken up to your True Nature already know, when a thing is very, very close to us (as in closer than close!) it can be really easy to overlook it. That's just what I did, so I'm here today to correct that.

Before we move into the "new" state, however, let me quickly address the idea of "stability." I have not seen anyone move from unconsciousness to stability in one leap, not in my own case, or in all the hundreds of cases where I have seen seekers awaken, or in any of the reports from awakened beings that I have personally talked to, never once. Count how many fingers I have up: Zero.

As a result of that sweeping and unopposed personal experience, I am going to completely remove "stability" from the short list of states immediately available upon awakening. I hear that it happens, but I hear about leprechauns and unicorns as well. So if it does, it's so rare that there's no point in discussing it. This teaching is always about the big numbers: what applies to the most people most of the time.

Though "stability" has been dropped, we are still left with two states, because the newly named state of "instability" now makes our list. Let me point out the difference between true oscillation and instability. I went from one to the other myself, but once again the shift was gradual, so I failed to note it.

Oscillation is the sense of movement between the dream and the truth, between fantasy and reality, between the direct knowledge of our True Nature and a state wherein one believes one has somehow lost, fallen out of, or been disconnected from our True

Nature. If it's any comfort to those of you presently in this state, let me say that regardless of how it feels or how it appears, this whole idea is patently untrue and could never for a moment be true.

"Then why am I so damn miserable?" I hear you ask.

To which I can only answer, "Because you're supposed to be until you're not. Hang in there."

Instability is the state of acceptance of apparent oscillation.

This is not a smarty-pants remark. Let me give you one example, although I've noticed a ton of them lately. It's like when you first learn a new word or buy a new car: suddenly you see the same word or car everywhere.

I have a student (self-declared) named Kathleen, who lives in the Midwest. I've watch Kathleen agonize and struggle through some apparently isolated but actually deeply spiritually integrated issues for the past year, and it makes my heart absolutely sing that she is living more freely today. Her husband is another self-declared student who woke up with me well over a year ago. Kathleen and I talk every couple of weeks and have become good friends, not just teacher and student. I haven't talked to her husband recently, but I hear he had a really good week as well, which makes me smile from ear to ear.

Kathleen has been talking to me once a month for about a year. I have to wonder if I didn't sense something coming, because right after our last conversation I suggested she go from once a month to twice a month, and as best I can recall I've never done that before. Kathleen saw the truth during our initial Awakening Session, but that brightness was almost instantly overcome by her chief story, which is the same as everybody else's chief story: "I, the victim."

Yet Kathleen never quit. She kept right on pushing right through her pain for a whole miserable year. And how's she doing right now? That's always the key, is it not? Well, I wrote her just as I started writing this article to tell her what I was doing, and she got right back in touch with me. I'm going to print her letter here, because she sums up the whole point of this post perfectly. Thank you, Kathleen.

Hey Fred,

Certainly, feel free to use my name, for this upcoming article and anytime in the future. I look forward to reading your article, especially because this instability is what I've been dealing with since my awakening. Not too surprising, since clarity is so new to me. I feel I'm being pulled between two worlds—the new truth and the old delusions. At first it caused some angst, but now I'm beginning to almost enjoy it. It's so interesting how I can dwell in two very different worlds!

Sometimes I'm light and bright. Nothing is real. There are just these beautiful perceptions playing in consciousness, energized by love, joy, bliss. And then I'll fall back in the "Bleh...help, so many terrifying and freaky things in this concrete reality!"

It's such a relief to know that the new reality is the "real" one. The old delusions still have momentum. I think they're afraid of this change. They are doing their best to hold onto me.

When delusion arises, I practice accepting it with love. I don't try to drive it away; I notice that just creates suffering. Rather, I practice opening up to the light of truth that is all around. And it flows in.

I'm grateful for my experience of recovery from addiction. I think that gives a very helpful road map for the experience of awakening. Although sobriety gives us a new and wonderful clarity, and can feel exhilarating, especially in the early days it's still not easy. Our old alcoholic identity struggles fiercely to pull us back, and we have to have faith and courage to forge ahead.

So I feel this same dynamic happening here. Clarity is wonderful, but my old identities and delusions are putting up a fight! But I know it will get easier as I practice abiding in awareness.

I hope you are doing great. I really look forward to reading your article.

All love,

Kathleen

If you are reading this and have had an awakening but now find yourself apparently estranged from Oneness, this your homework assignment is to follow Kathleen's advice:

"When delusion arises, I practice accepting it with love. I don't try to drive it away; I notice that just creates suffering. Rather, I practice opening up to the light of truth that is all around. And it flows in."

If cloudiness shows up, and we resist it, guess what we're doing? Resisting What Is, as it is, in this present moment. The thing that causes the sense of separation both before and after awakening is the same: Resisting What Is, as it is, in this present moment. I'm not asking you to surrender; you couldn't do that if you wanted to. What I'm suggesting is that you be open to being surrendered. "

Don't fight oscillation. Notice oscillation. When you fight it, guess who's fighting it? Ego. When you simply notice it and then go on with what you're doing, or better yet, do as Kathleen does and welcome it, you will move from suffering into the Great Okayness immediately. When you're in oscillation, you're in the fire. When you're experiencing blessed instability, you're warming up in front of the fire. Except of course, when you're not.

THE CONSCIOUSNESS EXPLOSION

Most of you will know by now that this teaching does not in any way dismiss, bypass, or otherwise minimize everyday life. Regardless of what may ultimately prove to be real or true, this is nonetheless our experience. And as such, it counts.

Consider the game of chess for a moment. The rules of chess are rigid and all-important—within the game. Without the rules there is no game. Yet outside of the game, the rules mean nothing. Within context, they count. We abide by them if we want to have any fun.

Yet if you and I take a turn at chess, what happens in our game doesn't genuinely matter. Either way, the sun will come up in the morning, clouds will form in the pristine sky, and millions of pink flamingos in Kenya will fly from their roosts without knowing, caring, or being affected by our pastime. Context is a big deal, like the outline of a picture in a coloring book. You don't have to color within the outline, but if you do, the picture is likely to be pleasing to more than just the person who colored it.

I've said all that as a setup to telling you about what does matter. Waking up matters. At the end of the day, in a human life that includes waking up, it is the only thing that matters. A human life that doesn't include it, in the end, is effectively incidental. It's neither here nor there. Mind you, they all count; please recall our context—I'm not talking trash about your dear mother.

But please, let's at least start to tell ourselves the truth. It's estimated that approximately 100,000,000,000 people inhabited this planet prior to us coming along. Yes, that's nine trailing zeroes, so we are talking a hundred billion. Add in our current cranky crop of seven billion more, and you've got yourself a pretty big number.

That's 107,000,000,000 human being thingies who from papoose to grave have believed they were the center of the universe.

Which one do you think is right about that claim? Ah yes, just one, of course. You. And here I was thinking it was me. How silly of me.

Wikipedia bothers to offer a line, paragraph, or page of record for somewhere around two million out of all those billions. It's a tiny, tiny percentage, but it's still a big number, and I admire Wikipedia for keeping up with even that many heroes and villains.

However, I notice that I am not among them. And unless you are Julius Caesar or Barack Obama, you probably are not either. So much for our claims to greatness, I guess. We are geologically insignificant, like a gnat on a dinosaur. As philosopher Greg Goode once told me, "People come, people go—that's showbiz!"

And for the sake of that single errant belief that we are the center of the universe, we gnats are home wreckers, a denotation made even worse when you notice that we are wrecking our own home.

Love, power, sex, money, and war all count, as do families, tribes, political borders, and mineral rights. We know they count, because we have effectively destroyed a planet over them. We have wiped out entire species of flora and fauna and turned forest, jungle, ocean, and mountains into vast wastelands of blight in order that we might get our scarce and sacred "piece of the rock."

It's all about me and mine: what I want, need, and even "deserve" in order to be safe, secure, and sexy—in order to be dominant-by-comparison, no matter what the arena or cost to others or to the earth. We are slaughtering all of our generations of babies to come in the name of sparkles, bells, and meaningless pissing contests. We are, as a species, insane. Not just insane, but dangerously insane. Strangely insane. Madly, wildly, incurably insane.

And this, my friends, is why waking up matters. I may sound like Chicken Little, but so be it. We are in the midst of a global emergency. Right now. What we do now counts. What we do now matters. It simply isn't all about us and ours. Will we realize that every species on the planet, including ours, is contingent upon what we do in the coming few years?

Despite what some may say, and I bless them for paying attention where we have not, it's not yet too late for planet Earth. We're in overtime, but the game ain't over just yet. Do you know how I know that? Because the cure is already here.

You are it. I am it. The enlightenment-centered spiritual community as a whole is it. We did it. Now we have to start undoing it. Which leaves us with the question of how we start undoing it.

First things first. Albert Einstein sagely said, "We can't solve problems by using the same kind of thinking we used when we created them." This is our issue. The bottom line is that we are ruining this beautiful, blue-green ball of hydrogen, oxygen, and carbon because of our belief in separation. It's as simple as that: it really is.

Just as in the quest for enlightenment, we can't see the truth because we won't tell ourselves the truth. Won't, not can't. Won't. The problem and the solution share the same address: ours. It's staring us in the face and we're looking everywhere but here, in our own mirrors.

I'm not saying the solution is as easy and chummy as everyone holding hands and singing "Kumbaya," but I am suggesting that in the absence of a significant number of awakened leaders and citizens there will be precious little to sing about. It starts with calling a spade a spade, with telling ourselves the truth about Oneness.

There's just One no-thing going on here. That truth is what this entire community is built around. So here's the good part. Here's where you come in.

Given that you're reading this line, the odds range from good to wonderful that if you are not already awake, then you will wake up to one level of clarity or another, and that you'll do it relatively soon. And therein lies the rub. What does "relatively soon" mean? I don't know, but it better be pretty quick if it's going to happen in time for you to aid Mother Nature, I know that much.

Lots of people are waking up. In 2001, a few years prior to its rolling across the planet like a tsunami, I got my first copy of *The Power of Now*. Someone on the Internet had told me about it. You couldn't buy a copy of it in Columbia, SC, and I didn't have a credit card in those rough old days, so Betsy bought it for me in Asheville, NC.

If you go to Barnes & Noble now, you'll see an Eckhart shelf. Byron Katie is traveling in disguise in the self-help section: the store is never without a copy of Katie's *A Course in Miracles*, which is a good and useful nondual book, I don't care what you say. The basic Buddha-books are all there and of course some books on Christian mysticism.

To my shock, I once discovered a copy of one of Ramesh Balsekar's books in Barnes & Noble! Talk about a lost child. I'm not fooling myself: it was a special order gone without pickup and put out for sale with a prayer, I guarantee it. Still, it made for a bright day for me. Barnes & Noble is a whole other world than what it was fifteen years ago.

47

Now, from this seat, in what is still the buckle of the Bible belt, where my potential victims are painfully short, I have nonetheless woken up a large handful, and I have a couple of folks who regularly come to see me.

And of course, from this same seat I get to watch people elsewhere wake up several times a week. I'm no longer just reading about it or dreaming about it. I'm living it, day in and day out, and even making my living at it. This is a full blown, Jesus-class miracle.

And everywhere I turn on the Internet there's a new book, website, or budding teacher. The world really is changing, and it's changing fast. Awakening is sort of like an international epidemic, only instead of people trying to avoid the carriers, everyone's trying to squeeze in close to them. "Me too! Me too!"

But up until now, evidence for sweeping change that Arjuna Ardagh wrote about in 2010 in *The Translucent Revolution* and which I spoke of in the introduction to *Beyond Recovery* in 2012, has been chiefly anecdotal instead of scientific. But perhaps that is changing.

Right after the close of this year's Science and Nonduality Conference, I got an email from The Center for the Study of Non-Symbolic Consciousness. The center is headed up by a guy who's very well-known and respected in our community, Dr. Jeffery A. Martin. Dr. Martin has been at the forefront of what I call "academic Nonduality" for years, having worked with former seekers, spiritual teachers, and universities around the world, establishing something of a protocol for researching persistent non-symbolic experiences (PNSE), what you and I would call enlightenment.

For more than eight years, Jeffery has traveled the world working with universities on establishing protocols for studying consciousness as an academic discipline, as well as interviewing hundreds of awakened beings, while meeting thousands of others, along with a host of spiritual teachers, many of whom you'd recognize.

Recently, while attending and participating in this year's Science and Nonduality Conference (SAND), Dr. Martin happened to hear about my track record in waking people up in a single session. He was intrigued, hence the email I received a few days later from his team. They spoke of this teaching (and six others) finding a potential audience of tens of thousands through something they called "The Finders Course," which is based on the knowledge gained in his massive research. That "tens of thousands" number got my attention in a big way, and I let them know that by return mail.

The following day, Dr. Martin and one of his colleagues, Nichol Bradford, and I got together in a Google Hangout video session and talked for more than two hours. There was instant chemistry and immediate understanding among us. The three of us left that meeting as friends. I was sold, and essentially they were too, but they needed to see samples of my work. No problem.

A few days later I was hosting a group Clarity Session via Zoom, and they attended it. It was the first video session I'd ever hosted where there were more than two people in attendance. We had some kind of funny little technical problems at the beginning (and damn it, I forgot to record it), but all that got ironed out quite quickly, and so far as I know, we all had a terrific experience for ninety minutes instead of the scheduled hour, which was no problem for me because I love working live—nothing keeps one alert and on one's toes quite the way a microphone does. Plus, of course, I'm a ham. It's my unit—don't blame me.

Half an hour after that meeting was over I met with a friend of Dr. Martin's who was not yet awake. She and I met for three hours, and when we parted, she was awake. And I was in. Rather than go into details, let me say that our discussion has, in short, been about taking enlightenment teachings to the masses. We are talking about preaching to those who, unlike yourself, are not already in the "nondual choir."

I will be helping the Center accomplish that mission in any way I can. This I do with an eye to, well, changing the world. I've said since the beginning that The Living Method of Awakening has the potential to turn the world on its head. I'm happy to now be involved in a project that may speed that along.

Last month I had an email from a nice, artist sort of guy who was headed out of the country, and he was hoping I might be able to squeeze him in for an Awakening Session before he left in just a few days. I made arrangements to do that, but then he back-pedaled, citing practical problems that might arise if he woke up. He promised to call me upon his return. Just as soon as he took care of the important stuff, he was sure he'd have time to pursue awakening.

And you? Save your planet. Save your descendants. Wake up. Wake up. Wake up. Now.

THE ONE THING WE GOTTA GIVE UP

I had a very long and difficult Awakening Session on Skype recently, less than 24 hours after another one just as tough. There is an energy exchange that takes place during these meetings, and it can be considerable. All sessions have the potential to tire the body: two tough ones in a row will positively drain me. The great news is that both of the clients in these sessions woke up. There's a reason for that. They knew they were asleep and they wanted to wake up.

The funny thing is that while the two guys were otherwise as different as night and day, their spiritual stories were very similar. Both of them had been around Nonduality for the last ten years. One guy reported that he'd read about a hundred books, and the second reported that he'd read even more, hundreds. Both had a head chock full of knowledge about this field, but neither one had the prize Kewpie doll to show for all that effort. Awakeness was not functioning consciously through either one of those units. These guys knew so damn much that there was no room to put anything new.

If you want real results, then you first have to come to me or any other teacher with an empty cup. There is a well-worn Zen story about that very thing, which shows that the already-full-cup has been a common seeker's malady for a long while. I deal with it all the time in various degrees. I had already seen this malady once earlier in the week, only that case was much worse than that of my two weekend guys. That client would not give up the one thing that's an absolute must and consequently is not awake.

That client was full of knowledge and was suffering from the delusion of being already awake. This, my friends, is death. If we suffer from this malady, it's the one thing we gotta give up. But how can I be sure that somebody's got this problem?

People who have woken up with me in an Awakening Session know better than to try and bullshit me. When someone wakes up, then I am suddenly in conversation with myself. I know when I'm talking to myself, and I know when I'm not. There's no faking it, not for very long.

But what about someone who's been through an Awakening Session with me but did not wake up? They know what that shift is all about, so they'll think they can fool me. They think wrong, but why would anyone even attempt such a thing? Two reasons: arrogance and ignorance.

Such clients want to have graduated from "common spirituality." They want to impress me, or someone else, or amazingly enough, themselves. They have their own spiritual model, and this teaching doesn't match it. These clients don't want to wake up on Life's terms, only on their own. Awakening rarely happens like that folks, and awakening is NEVER what we think it is. And on and on...

I don't see this too often, but once in a while it will raise its ugly head, and last week was one of those times. Yuck.

If you come to me full and are willing to tell yourself the truth about it, as my recent back-to-back clients were, then most of the time I can help you empty your cup prior to beginning our session. But if you come to me full, yet sporting a face of false humility that's been sculptured into the guise of someone who is empty, then I won't know to help you prior to our session. You'll then sit there for two or two-and-half hours answering questions from your head instead of your heart. I'll figure out what's going on, trust me on that, but my job is only to wake up those who want to wake up.

This client did not want to wake up and seemed to think my job was to convert them. As a result, this client is not awake and is on the most perilous territory that exists in this game, standing a wonderful chance of never waking up. I hope my client reads this and recognizes who I'm writing about. Maybe that will start the alarm clock ringing. It's unlikely, but at least it's possible. I always like to tell myself the most pleasant story available, provided it's not going to cause me to live stupidly.

When someone engages me to help them meet their True Nature, I take that very, very seriously. I'll try every trick in my book to bring that about, and I have quite a few. I will back up and go through some of the same material a second, a third, even a fourth time. I will let the session run long, and by the way I charge by the session, not by the hour. I will use material that most people never hear, because they don't need it, or it won't benefit them.

I will be sweet. I will be funny. I will even try to talk down a mild skeptic if he or she is pleasant enough, a duty which can be rather annoying. I will also raise my voice, wave my arms, and badger a client all to hell and back if that's what's required. There's nothing personal in it; The Living Method meets everyone where they really are, not in the Never Never Land of where they "should be." I don't even do what I do. It just happens.

I simply don't operate on the assumption that you want me to wake you up but only if I can do it in a kinder gentler "spiritual" way. I know how badly I wanted it, and if you'd convinced me that giving me two black eyes and a bloody nose would wake me up, I promise I would have asked you to please wale away. So the gloves are off, and whatever it takes until it takes is okay with me. My preference is that every session be light and funny and end up with the client in brilliant clarity, but this is not about my preferences—or yours.

So, in the end, I beg of you, give up the one thing you gotta give up—ahead of time, if possible. Be up front with your teacher; this is not a competition. I don't actually care how awake or asleep you are so long as it doesn't interfere with my work. Check yourself. If you're legitimately wondering if you're awake or not, check out "So, Am I Awake Yet or What?" in *The Book of Unknowing* or the version on my website *Awakening Clarity Now*. You'll find some good pointers in that article.

It's not about these units. That notion is just more self-centered dreaming, not Self-focused living. The following comments sum up what awakening is really all about. The writer, Barbara, is now ready to joyfully serve her Self regardless of what shows up for the unit.

> *I've had the good fortune to attend two "Awakening" & two "Clarity" sessions with Fred. The first set was one-on-one, and the most recent was with a group of over a dozen people. In all four, Fred skillfully took me on a journey that showed who I am. When that seeing happens, even for one minute, it sets off a new dynamic of un-doing. The most recent Awakening session left no room for doubt or longing. I don't care if I see clearly or not. The Knowing of who I am is*

indisputable so it's easier when the clouds form. Abiding and Non-abiding may be a dualistic concept. Now I can begin to Love what is when it's clear or cloudy.

Sincerely,

Barbara
Fairview, NC

THE BLIND MEN AND THE NONDUAL ELEPHANT

Most of us already know the famous story of the blind men and the elephant. For those who don't or who've forgotten, here's my edited version of the *Wikipedia* entry about it.

The Tale Itself

In various versions of the tale, a group of blind men (or men in the dark) touch an elephant to learn what it is like. Each one feels a different part, but only one part, such as the side or the tusk. They then compare notes and learn that they are in complete disagreement. The stories differ primarily in how the elephant's body parts are described, how violent the conflict becomes and how (or if) the conflict among the men and their perspectives is resolved. In some versions, they stop talking, start listening and collaborate to "see" the full elephant. When a sighted man walks by and sees the entire elephant all at once, they also learn they are blind.

The Lesson

The story of the blind men and an elephant originated in the Indian subcontinent from where it has widely diffused. It has been used to illustrate a range of truths and fallacies; broadly, the parable implies that one's subjective experience can be true, but that such experience is inherently limited by its failure to account for other truths or a totality of truth. This applies even in the case of the sighted man. If he were deaf, for example, he would not hear the elephant trumpet. At various times the parable has provided insight into the relativity, opacity, and inexpressible nature of truth.

As I See It

It occurred to me recently that this tale wonderfully illustrates the current nondual spiritual marketplace. Each of the blind men is an archetypal seeker. Each has already "got hold of" a part of Reality, and they are all trying to experience the whole thing. In the background, like a Shakespearean Chorus, is a group of spiritual teachers who are shouting encouragement and pointers. These are good teachers, are themselves clear, and are calling out everything they can think of to aid the blind men.

However, every single one of the blind men thinks that every pointer he hears called out is especially for him, so they move around in an excited circle, constantly changing positions, grabbing this, squeezing that, trying all sorts of stuff, but still never experiencing the whole elephant. They "dig a hundred shallow holes" but never a single deep one.

These seekers have confused activity with progress. It's a common confusion. A hamster may be endlessly engaged in the activity of turning its wheel, but it's not making any actual progress. Our seekers are collecting more and more ideas about the elephant, but once again, the end goal is as elusive as ever—nobody's really getting anywhere.

The Nondual Twist

There is a special version of the elephant story that's reserved particularly for those of us involved in Nonduality. You may not have heard this twist, so I'll go ahead and share it. In the nondual version of this story, the blind men are not actually blind. They simply have their eyes closed and are pretending to be blind. Some of the teachers are even hollering out for them to open their eyes. This is the one pointer that's meant for everyone, yet it's the one pointer the blind men ignore. Why don't they open their eyes? Because they think they're blind!

Somewhere along the way each of them witnessed a thought that said, "You're blind," and rather than allowing that thought arise and fall harmlessly, they caught hold of it. Each of them declared this empty, universal thought to be their thought. This declaration makes this thought feel important to them and perhaps more significantly trustworthy. After all, your thoughts are all suspect, but my thoughts? Gospel, every single one of them.

We always believe what we think we are thinking—provided it's negative, of course. We know we can't trust the rising thoughts that tell us foolishness like:

All is well.

I'm okay as I am.

It'll all work out in the end.

We ignore these thoughts in favor of the ones that are already going around in our heads, the ones that say, "Something's gone wrong and it's just going to get worse—especially for me." Now there is a trustworthy thought. "Doom is right around the corner, I'm sure of it." Ahhhhhh. We're used to suffering, so now we're back in our comfort zone.

The Traps

In working with hundreds of clients, and having gone through this whole process myself, I've found a multitude of "reasons" why people are not awake right now. I'm presenting the four that are at the top of the list, but they are by no means all of them. There's plenty where these came from.

1. The Insistence that My Character Come to the Awakening Party

Every client I've ever had has been caught in this endless loop, and I was as well. If you're not awake right now, you are caught in it too—I guarantee it. The desire to take the character to the Awakening Party is

one of the key "reasons" that people who come to me are not already experiencing Reality As It Is, which is the same reason I didn't until I did.

I believed that Fred should be allowed at that blessed event. After all, good old Fred had for so many years put in so much time, effort, money and attention (notice the combination of an entitlement and victim story), that it was only right that Fred should be allowed to attend, complete with pointy hat and party whistle.

There was, however, a fatal flaw in that story. The moment that Fred shows up at the Awakening Party, the party is over. The presence of Fred guarantees the absence of Conscious Awakeness. And the presence of Conscious Awakeness guarantees the absence of Fred. We can have this cake or that cake but just like Momma told us, "We can't have our cake and eat it too." The thing that wants to walk across the graduation stage and pick up its diploma—for all the world to see—never will.

2. The Precious Victim Story

Most and maybe all people also have a version of the victim story—the difference is only a matter of degree. The unwillingness to let it go of this "I've been wronged/they did this and that to me/what I'm going through isn't right" is a guarantee of continued delusion. We want to keep this story more than we want to wake up to Truth. Until we don't. At that point, instead of asking "Why me?" we'll graduate to the true position of "Why not?" And, as an important note, let me add that our victim story can even extend to our spiritual story, so be alert.

3. The Story of Being Right

Once again, the need to "be right" is almost universal. And once again, it's nearly impossible for the mind to get the mind out of it. First off, few of us lack the sheer willingness to give this up. Secondly, we don't have the objectivity. And third, we simply don't know the truth.

And ALL of these "reasons" fall under a single heading, which is that we are believing thoughts. We are believing thoughts, and we are not yet ready to "unbelieve" them. The bottom line is that we are unwilling—at this moment—to tell ourselves the truth. We want to stay in our story more than we want to wake up. There's nothing inherently wrong with that. We do until we don't.

Everyone reading this has either already told themselves the truth or is well on the way to doing so. You don't end up here by happenstance. Many who tell themselves the truth will then fall back into denial—I did any number of times. That's okay, too. It is what it is until it isn't. Lose any guilt, shame, or blame about your "spiritual behavior" or your "present spiritual condition." They are absolutely without value.

Let's do realize that when I suggest you are "close" that I'm speaking of what I call "the package"—DNA patterns, memories, habits, desires, etc.—that clearly move up the line from one unit to another. We can trace both your DNA and mine back to ancient Africa, so this is neither guesswork nor mysticism. This is science. Something moves. So, given that "your package" has been on the path for thousands of years, you can "have your head in tiger's mouth" and still not wake up for 200 years. Everybody eventually will, but I'd take little personal comfort from that.

You might want to lend yourself a hand.

And don't fool yourself; don't wait for that Special Invitation to Awaken to arrive via the Virgin Mary. We have all already received the invitation any number of times. Up until now, most of us have said, "No." Awakeness CAN override a "No," but it rarely will. Still, place no limitations on Awakeness. It is beyond imagination, beyond the mind, beyond logic.

4. The Lifestyle Trap

As we become long-term seekers, then the people we allow ourselves to get really close to are also often long-term seekers. And we all make a silent agreement. "Since none of us really expect to wake up anymore anyway, let's make spirituality our end and not our means. But let's do it right. Let's wear flowy clothes, go vegetarian, and enjoy some retreats in exotic locations. Cool. And deadly.

Even if we do happen to have an awakening, if we're not willing to go our own way, to walk our own often solitary path, then we may have a social problem. We broke the rules, we shattered the Silent Code. We woke up, and that's just not cool. Now you don't fit in with your friends any longer. Not only will they not care about your awakening, few if any will even believe you. However, if you act swiftly enough, you can deny your awakening and try to fit back in. There will be some who are disgruntled, but eventually the wound will heal, and you'll be back at the art openings with all the rest of the chic spiritual crowd. Even if you're sharing a remote desert tent with a bunch of ardent seekers, the same resocialization can happen, so don't think it's just a "California thing."

Getting Past the Traps

This is how I make a living. In Awakening Sessions, one of the key things I have to do is figure out the client's blocks. What thoughts are coming up that the client is believing? What story are they telling themselves? Why have they heretofore been unwilling to tell themselves the truth? How can I best make the truth of how things are so incredibly clear—for them—that they'll be unable to turn their head from it? How can I best help them come to see the Most Obvious Thing, help snap them out of the divine hypnosis that's keeping them from noticing That Which Can't Be Missed? This is why it's The Living Method of Awakening. Every client is different, and so is every session.

Speaking of believing our thoughts, here's one of the most revered: it's always been implied—often stated outright—that coming to recognize our True Nature is quite difficult. If we find ourselves drawn to that quest, then collective wisdom will direct us toward some mystical tradition—Sufism, Zen, Advaita Vedanta, Christian mysticism, or what have you. And to join that tradition is mostly thought to be the beginning of a long, nearly impossible path. Maybe that was once so, and maybe it's still so for almost all of the world. But I can state with absolute confidence that for the great majority of the people who are attracted to this teaching, coming to recognize your true nature is just not that difficult. Either it's not or I'm a fraud: it's just that simple. Because every week, five or six days a week, I'm out there in the Wi-Fi world helping people come to see who they are. No problem.

The challenge is in getting people to accept what they see, because most of the people in this crowd have seen their True Nature at one time or another, perhaps many times. And then, damn it, it just went away. The next day, we're not even sure if it really happened. Back to the cushion we go. "Maybe next time I'll really get it!"

The Living Method Solution

Asking the mind to free you from the mind is simply asking too much. It ain't gonna happen. That doesn't mean one can't wake up by luck or grace, but let's tell ourselves the truth about how often that happens. Chances are strong that it hasn't happened to you, or if it did it has since passed. There's a lot to be said for abidance.

What I've discovered over the past two years is that almost nobody will tell themselves the truth about Truth if they can avoid it—even if they want to wake up. Thus, in an Awakening Session I arrange things so that you essentially can't avoid the truth. A small percentage manage to hold firm in denial, but not many. So what actually happens? We start with the idea that almost nobody will accept who they really are until they have first seen to their own satisfaction what they are not. So through a series of inquiries and investigations that last about 90 minutes, we do neti neti (not this, not that) on steroids. In the Christian tradition this is known as via negativa—the negative way. I imagine some of the other great traditions have a similar path for the contrary seeker.

Once you know what you are not, I've found that there's a short window of opportunity for me to present what you are. The Truth is nearly always seen and is then accepted on a sliding scale, the scale being contingent upon the willingness of the client to tell themselves the truth. Very often the openings are quite clear, sometimes amazingly clear, and sometimes less clear.

The point of the exercise is to at least glimpse the whole elephant. Once it has been seen, few will go back to blindly grabbing trunks and tails.

WHEN INTELLECT OUTPACES EXPERIENCE

An intellectual command of nondual precepts may create quite a clear concept of what one is looking for, but that concept is not always helpful. Worse yet, this general understanding may even seem like Awakeness itself. Now, before we get too hasty in condemning intellect, long-term readers mine will know that I am not one to minimize the value of intellect on the nondual path. Far from it. Intellect is the underpinning which functions as a foundation for all that comes afterward. Without it we are pretty much nowhere in this field, but at some point we have to go beyond it.

My clients, without exception, are smart people easily able to understand nonduality from an intellectual angle. I can't say for certain that such is the case for everyone who follows this teaching online or through my books, but I'd be willing to bet it's pretty durn close. I'm not trying to puff everybody up. I just want to present an accurate view of the intellectual ecosystem in which The Living Method operates.

We could say that this teaching is a form of jnana yoga, which is the intellectual path to freedom, as opposed to bhakti yoga (devotion) and karma yoga (selfless works). Jnana yoga may sometimes attract nonintellectuals, but they will not stay. This approach to freedom via intellect doesn't make jnana inherently better than other paths, but it certainly does make it more direct. In this teaching it also makes it much faster, more reliable, and more predictable. But that's only because my clients have already done most of my work for me. They've managed to wear the seeker out through thinking to the point that they are ready to tell themselves the truth.

But what happens after awakening? What happens to all of

that intellectual seekerism? Let me report my own experience first. Those of you who know this part please bear with me or skip ahead.

If I discount a very clear but short glimpse back in 1992, then my first major awakening was in 2006. It was clear and durable. Yet the further I got away from "the moment," the less clear it got. First it closed down from the fresh immediate experience of being Oneness to the experience of the witness state. I see this all the time in clients and would say it is the most common course that initial awakening takes. In my case, the witness deteriorated further to what felt like merely the memory of Oneness. This sense of Oneness "remembered" is very common but also very problematic.

The chief issue is that mind, with its quite limited capacity, cannot contain Awakeness. If you think about it for a minute, it just makes sense that mind cannot encompass that which it is encompassed by. This is why you cannot possibly, ever, ever, no exceptions, think your way into enlightenment. What we can do is use the mind to go beyond the mind, which is what I do in every Awakening Session, so the mind's contribution is great, but in the end it is limited.

The other problem with the notion of ever capturing Awakeness in memory is that in order to remember something we have to have a "rememberer." By the time the "spiritual experience" aspect of my awakening was a month or two in the past, I had unknowingly started taking a bit of a nap and had reverted to thinking of myself as a noun-named-Fred who now possessed High Mystical Knowledge. Although actual brightness had passed, the "rememberer" of the awakening, the ultimately illusory-yet-deluded Fred character was quite proud of himself. Mind had rebuilt ego.

It was at this stage that I ran all my non-nondual friends away by being insufferable. And it wasn't long before I ended up doing some reseeking. Imaginary Fred moved into misidentification, commonly known as oscillation, and it became Imaginary Fred's job to "get back" the brightness that Imaginary Fred thought he had once possessed but had somehow lost. The problem there is that I had now assigned the finding of a solution for Fred's oscillation over to the cause of my oscillation: Fred.

If you haven't experienced oscillation yet, you may not understand that last sentence very well. If you have, you are probably pumping your fist in the air and crying, "YES! THAT'S IT

EXACTLY!" I really should have bought myself a T-shirt at the time that read, "Fred Is An Awakening Survivor!"

Let us assume that you've had an experience of brightness but that the experience waned. Now, thanks be to the gods, there's the feeling that you are beginning to clear again. How do we know what's real and what's intellect telling itself a story, a particularly detailed authentic-sounding story about what awakening was or is? Mind is always happy to tell itself a new tale, particularly if it ends up aggrandizing ego.

Here are some pointers a friend of mine sent in when he suggested I write this article.

1. If you're asking yourself, "Am I awake?" then the odds are that you're not. If you've had a true (confirmed, if possible) awakening, the pertinent question is "Am I clear?"
2. The second pointer is a follow-up to the first: you're not going to be able to answer the question "Am I clear?" from your head. You know how reporters are always saying that they got such and such information from a "reliable source?" Well, when it comes to judging your own clarity, your mind will not be a "reliable source," at least not for a long time. By the time it's become reliable you'll find out that you don't need it for this task after all.
3. You are reacting to people differently. In the end, we each get a single choice in this life, and we don't even have that one until we've advanced through the Gateless Gate. Once we have, however, we get to make this choice over and over and over, in every single moment as we take in every new arising. That choice is, "Where am I going to see this from?" If you look from the eyes of truth (meaning you look through that unit, and not as that unit), you will see people differently, more as aspects of yourself, and your actions regarding them will change accordingly.
4. You are reacting differently to life situations, that is, to the content of your life. If a tree branch falls on your car, for example, you are less outraged. The event seems more like just one of those things and less like a personal attack on you by malevolent nature.

Note that these changes regarding people and situations take time to fully embed, as in years. And no, you do not get to skip ahead a grade, not even special you, or special me for that matter. The examples are nearly endless, but I think these four will serve for now.

Meister Eckhart, Christian mystic of the 13th and 14th centuries, said "People want to see God with their own eyes, the way they see a cow." This is the way of the intellect. Alas, we cannot, because that which is seeing the cow is not other than the cow.

We can only see God through God's eyes. Our mind can lead us to the brink, but in the end we must follow the Way of the Heart, which calls for a seeing that goes beyond the mind.

WHAT'S TAKING ALL THIS ACTION?

One of the questions I get regularly and which I consistently ask of myself is "What's really going on here? Who's doing this or that—little me or Big I? This question seems to make sense, and on one level it does. I try to watch out for egoic action on the part of Fredness that seems to be chiefly for the advancement of Fredness—and I never have to wait long.

Yessiree, there is still egoic movement taking place through the unit that's typing this article. I know it's a so-called spiritual teacher, and it's supposed to be a bona fide awake being, but that doesn't make it an exception to ordinary human pitfalls. In fact, it may make it even more prone to error. Let's not fool ourselves: I can see it, you can see it, a blind man on Mars can see it, so why deny it? Yet the actions I'm referring to, and which we'll go into a little later, are not entirely egoic—I would go so far as to say they are not even primarily egoic, so let's withhold judgment until we've done a bit of investigation.

What I'm specifically talking about is that I have been regularly hammered about the self-promoting nature of this character ever since it left my living room three-and-a-half years ago in an attempt to get this counter-intuitive, radical teaching out of my house and into the world.

And you know what? On one level it's justified criticism. Guilty, guilty, guilty. I have indeed promoted this teaching—and thus the character who appears to be behind it—at every opportunity. I never met a microphone I didn't like or a connected individual with whom I wouldn't do a little schmoozing. This behavior may appear unenlightened, it may be lame, or even disgusting to some. It may be something we should all try to avoid. But you know what else? It's been really, really effective.

In the summer of 2011, I was, in the parlance we tend to use, an "awake guy" sitting in my living room with a strong pull to do something, but I didn't know what to do or how to do it. I'd always been a good writer, but there was no way I was going to sit down and write a book on spec in the hope that it might miraculously find a publisher. I'd been around the publishing field too long to go that route. I knew the odds, and I simply was not willing to play. Nor was I clear on what it was that I specifically wanted to share. At that time, I didn't really have anything new to offer—The Living Method didn't yet exist, and there were plenty of good nondual books already on the market, so why simply put out another me-and-my-awakening title?

When I started the original *Awakening Clarity* blog, I was very excited. I'm an enthusiastic guy anyway, and a project like this was enough to push me up the scale from my normal level of eight all the way to ten and a half.

There was only one problem. Other than Betsy, I was the only person in the world who knew I had a new, nondual-oriented website. And we were the only two who cared. I could see no point in having a blog without an audience, so I started promoting, and promoting, and promoting—and I have yet to stop. I do it because it works, not because I'm actually keen on it. I honestly hope there will come a time when I can stop promoting and rest from all of that stuff, but it ain't that time just yet.

Has there been any ego tied up in promoting this teaching? Of course! Is there still? Of course! It looks to me like it's unavoidable until it isn't. Does it really matter? Everyone has their own opinion on this, but I don't think so.

As much as my inner promoter would love to believe differently, none of this is about Fred. Do you know how I know that? Because there is no Fred. That makes it pretty clear, don't you think? Does it sometimes feel like it's about Fred and not just the august teaching? Sure. It feels that way to both of us.

Do you think I don't know how ham-handed I can be at times? I know. I squirm in my chair, I think about some of the hail that's sure to fall on me, and then I press Publish anyway. It's what this unit does. For all I know, it's one of the reasons this teaching landed here. It sure wasn't my spotless karma, I promise you that. So, if being thought to be a totally arrogant, egoic, selfish, unenlightened, money-hungry, publicity-pumping fool by some people is what it takes to get out the message that liberation is available right here, right now—for you—then I'm game. Only the character would be keen about protecting itself from any of that. Awakeness couldn"t care less.

Ultimately, as I've already stated, there's no Fred here. The lights are on, but no one is home. It is only Awakeness that can be acting, because there is only Awakeness to act. If folks want to roast their Fredness projection, that's just fine. My projection sometimes cringes, so we're even. But Awakeness is all about efficiency and this sometimes quite uncomfortable-for-Fredness way of getting the job done is nonetheless getting the job done.

Lots and lots of people who don't know me don't like me. Cool! That's a sort of left-handed achievement, but it's still an achievement! It's not an achievement for anybody, but it's still an achievement. I put my back to the wall, take on all comers, and say "Send me money, I'll wake you up!"

Lots of people don't think I can do what I can do. So what? There are plenty enough who do think so to keep me busy for the foreseeable future. And there are tons of people who know I'm telling the truth. The proof's in the pudding, folks, and there's a lot of pudding out there—on six different continents.

On a lighter note, lots and lots of people who don't know me love me. Even cooler! Nowadays I get gratitude mail every single day from people all over the place thanking me for changing their lives with articles, books, and "look-at-me, look-at-me" wise-silly videos. That wasn't happening three-and-a-half years ago, I can tell you that. And it wouldn't be happening now, had Awakeness not been willing to sacrifice this character's "nondual cool" to the cause. I no longer belong to the Long-Faced, Serious-Talking Teacher's Club. Durn. It's not just a small price to pay; in the end, it's no price at all, because the Fred character is 100% fictional anyway!

Let me lay this out for us. So far, hundreds of people have gotten to wake up—and many of them had tried a whole lot of other ways to do so. This works. If I don't die anytime soon that number will easily climb into the thousands—and who knows, this teaching might carry on long after I die—I hope so. I'm working with several people right now who could end up being splendid teachers.

Conversely, one unreal character of no consequence— Fredness—has to occasionally writhe in embarrassment at his own egoic actions. My friends have to lower their eyes and whisper to each other "For God's sake, he's done it again. When is he going to learn?" My "enemies" have a new joke to share at the online water cooler at my expense. Okay!

It seems like a fair trade to me, but what do I know? After all, this Fredness is just a meta-pattern that appears to be the senior partner but in fact is not even riding herd on the vast collection of smaller patterns whirling underneath it. One has to assume that it must be a fair trade for Awakeness, given that it's calling all the shots anyway. It's what's happening; I'm pretty sure that's a mystical thumb's up.

I know that even though it makes no sense and is entirely paradoxical, it's somehow nonetheless critical for the Fred-who-doesn't-exist to cooperate with the inevitable-that-is. So you know what? I'm on board. Have at it, Awakeness. Spare me nothing that Truth requires. You're not going to anyway, but I'm "allowing" it. And thanks for all the rotten stuff that's helped me wake up, too. I wouldn't be here without it, even though it sucked out loud.

WAKING UP WITH YOUTUBE

This post concerns a particularly dear Letter from the Field. Many times, for different reasons, I have to keep Letters from the Field anonymous. It's wonderful not to have to do so here, and yes, I am shamelessly milking it for all it's worth. This unit does what it does; I'm not pulling those strings.

To my mind, it marks a key milestone in this teaching. It's dear to me not so much for what it says—although it is both kind and generous—but because of who says it. The author of the letter is Dr. Jenny Wade. I guess the easiest way to introduce her is by reprinting the short bio that appears on the website TranscendentSex.org.

> Dr. Jenny Wade is a lecturer, researcher, and consultant who specializes in the structuring of awareness, especially the spontaneous openings and intentional practices that expand human potential by accessing hidden or unused innate capacities. She is a developmental psychologist who studies processes that open gateways to greater possibility than is considered normal in everyday existence, but that is potentially available to all human beings.
>
> In addition to her research on unusual states of awareness, Dr. Wade's extensive research of variations in normal adult consciousness forms the basis of a leadership and organization development consulting practice. She has over twenty years' experience working with Fortune 500 companies and multinationals in a wide range of industries to optimize performance.
>
> Dr. Wade is the author of *Changes of Mind: A Holonomic Theory of the Evolution of Consciousness, Transcendent Sex: When Lovemaking Opens the Veil,*

and numerous articles. She is on the core faculty of the Institute of Transpersonal Psychology in Palo Alto. Dr. Wade is a keynote speaker, lecturer, and workshop leader.

Beyond her comments about her latest awakening experience, Jenny's letter also underscores the much-undervalued necessity of follow-up in the post-awakening "state." Time after time after time we think, "I've got it now! I can never unsee this!" What we don't realize is that at the exact moment we're saying that, we are announcing to the world, "Oh my God, there was such incredible clarity here and it's already gone!"

> *Dear Fred,*
>
> *I've been enrolled in the third cohort of Jeffery A. Martin's research study to evoke persistent non-symbolic experience (popularly enlightenment, liberation, non-duality), and this week's assignment was direct inquiry accompanied by a lot of video/ audio resources to help. Although I myself am a researcher of consciousness and had had a classic satori experience years ago as well as another occasion of being in non-duality for a couple of months, all of it had faded, hence his course. I didn't find [the pointers from a well-known teacher] or any of the other resources helpful until I stumbled onto yours on YouTube—and I was riveted.*
>
> *Your simplicity, directness, humor, rapscallion past, and oddball humility—and especially your southern accent, which is "home" to my ears—told how to get there better than anybody else I've come across in a long career, at least in a way that appealed to me. I immersed myself in your shorter videos (none more than 30 minutes), especially the one about intellecttualizing and the self-reflecting bubble, which spoke to the biggest problem I was having. And your words about denial in another video—and those brought me right home (Location 2, according to Jeffery) without any fanfare.*
>
> *I want to thank you and let you know how much your generosity has helped at least one other person. And to also express how helpful your work is on following up the experiences, which I know only too well can otherwise vanish entirely. Words aren't adequate to*

express my gratitude. If I can do anything to further your work, including providing an endorsement, please let me know.

Much love and esteem,

Jenny

Thank you Jenny. I'm enjoying our many conversations.

REBOUNDING FROM LIMBO

More and more people are coming to me who have had an "awakening experience" at some time in the past, whether a month ago or forty years ago, but who now know—or strongly suspect—that they are not presently awake. However, no "person" is ever awake, including Fred, but in recall it may feel like he or she was.

What we call "waking up" is an event or a number of events within an overall awakening process that was going on prior to the event and which will continue beyond that event's conclusion. It is a vertical spike appearing on a horizontal line. Quite simply, awakeness wakes up to the truth of itself and of its invention, the character it's playing, the Fred or Sue or Bob that it's pretending to be in order to experience itself objectively.

Herein lies the rub. As seekers, who are after all human units, we want to experience Oneness objectively; everybody does. That might be okay if we were not already experiencing Oneness objectively! When we are confused seekers, we are hoping to *reach* Oneness. Awakening is discovering that we *are* Oneness. We can't discover anything outside of Oneness in order to have an objective experience of it, so we are left with only subject. Objects merely appear to exist.

Everyday life, the dream, the movie, call it what you will, is not merely an experience that we as human beings are taking in. It can just as truly be said, even more truly said, that being human is an experience that Oneness is taking in by pretending to be a unit, by playing the role of our character.

When conscious awakeness begins to close back down after that initial spike of clarity, which is what happened to me and pretty much everyone I've ever worked with, memory will tell us that it was the character, in my case Fred, who woke up. It seems that Fred had something special, but then somehow he lost it, fell out of it, or forgot it. And since Fred lost it, guess whose job it is to "get it back?" That's right, it's Fred's job. This wouldn't be so much of a problem if there was a Fred hiding about somewhere, but there's not. Thus the belief in the one tasked with rediscovering awakening is in itself the only impediment to awakening.

Yes, it can be confusing. At the end of that round, we are left in a state where we are not consciously awake, yet neither are we where we were prior to the blessed/cursed event. We now know something in our heads, but we can't quite remember what it is. A footprint or imprint of awakening remains, but we are bereft of the thing itself. We are lost in limbo, and we can stay there indefinitely.

That we are in limbo can be a hard truth to tell ourselves, but there seems to be a creeping new willingness for rebounders to come forward and address their situation honestly. This is great news, because just as we rebounded from clarity back into cloudiness, so can we rebound back into clarity, and this time we might even stay there—mostly! True stability takes time, because the nature/nurture patterns of DNA and post-birth conditioning will roll on until they don't. My ceiling fan continues to turn even after I've cut it off, and so did my blind patterns. The unit does what it does until it doesn't.

I cannot say often enough that enlightenment is all about right now. What we have "seen" or "experienced" at some time in the past is essentially incidental. If we are not presently being that which was "seen" in the spiritual experience, that which the unit's memory thinks it accurately recalls, then we are not—pardon the phrase—an awake being. We are not dancing, we are being danced.

This arising—this very arising, precisely as it's being known—is the way that you are expressing yourself to yourself in this so-called moment. There's just one thing going on, and that happening just happens to be you. If we know this at this moment, then we are awake. If we do not, we are not.

Some of this is simply languaging. If I have a client who woke up with me a month or even a year ago, and they are not awake to the current arising, I may refer to them as "awake, but cloudy." By that I mean that conscious awakeness has stirred through that body and is now on "stand-by" instead of simply being "potentially conscious," which is the state of mankind generally. A potential flier can be miles from the airport. Somebody flying stand-by has the bags packed and is sitting at the airport awaiting a call. It's a big difference.

However, the more time that has elapsed between the Big Day and this day, the further we're probably going to find ourselves and our baggage from the boarding gate. I can, should it prove necessary, generally bring someone who was experiencing brightness two weeks ago "back to brightness" a lot faster than someone who woke up a year ago. The latter is probably going to entail a whole new Awakening Session; whereas, the former is likely to be just a matter of a few tweaks.

If we come to brightness and then dim, you can bet dimness is going to be painful. The longer you've been out of the dream, the tougher it's going to be. We may become like a drug addict, only instead of heroin, we're looking for another hit of clarity and possibly the bliss which may accompany it. This is thinking that the vertical spike is more spiritual than the horizontal line, which is simply circular conditioning running itself empty and then refueling itself. It'll happen until it doesn't.

I didn't step off the treadmill until I admitted that I was lost in limbo and found myself a teacher to help me escape.

WORKING WITH HEAVY KARMA

There is a circular phenomenon that occurs in addiction. One of the best comments on it can be found in "The Doctor's Opinion" section of *The Big Book* of Alcoholics Anonymous. Dr. William Duncan Silkworth writes:

> Men and women drink essentially because they like the effect produced by alcohol. The sensation is so elusive that, while they admit it is injurious, they cannot after a time differentiate the true from the false. To them, their alcoholic life seems the only normal one. They are restless, irritable and discontented, unless they can again experience the sense of ease and comfort which comes at once by taking a few drinks—drinks which they see others taking with impunity. After they have succumbed to the desire again, as so many do, and the phenomenon of craving develops, they pass through the well-known stages of a spree, emerging remorseful, with a firm resolution not to drink again. This is repeated over and over, and unless this person can experience an entire psychic change there is very little hope of his recovery.

What the good doctor is describing is a blind, or unconscious, pattern. It's a default conditioning, just like when I start up my computer and Windows, The Weather Channel, and my anti-virus software all open up. That will continue to happen until I either change the prompts or the computer dies.

In recovery, we have a saying that runs, "If you sober up a horse thief, you'll have yourself a sober horse thief." In other words, you may have removed the crazy juice from that body, but you haven't removed the crazy thinking from that brain. That takes time. Those of you who are already awake as you read this will know that neither the unit nor the personality wakes up in a so-called awakening. Awakeness wakes up to itself. Given that the character-unit doesn't wake up, guess what? It keeps doing much of what it was doing before it woke up!

We call this "dancing out the dance." The unit will do what it does until it does something else. We wake up to the dream, but we do not wake up from the dream. Once awakening occurs, however, we can begin to witness our life patterns. Some will be skillful, many will not be.

But through witnessing these patterns, by simply noticing them and being willing to be other than the way we are, which is often the hardest part, these patterns will begin to fade. Once we fully penetrate a pattern, seeing absolutely clearly that this is no longer beneficial, then that pattern will drop you. You don't drop it, it drops you. This can take some repetition. Go easy on yourself during this phase. I'm 8+ years in, and I'm still in this phase. It's all a matter of degree.

We could call these patterns karma. We could in fact call DNA itself karma. It's the residual stuff that somehow moves up the unit line. We know it does, because we can trace every single one of our DNA lines back to Africa thousands of years ago. And what is DNA? A collection of patterns.

Ramana Maharshi said that there are three types of karma in post-awakening. The first is "carved-in-stone" karma, meaning that this karma is already cast, and it's going to play out in the world, enlightenment or no, and that is that. For example, you've been speeding down the same road, 60 mph in a 35 zone, for the last five years of your pre-awakening. On Monday you wake up, everything is perfect, and then traveling 60 you skid out in the rain, hit a tree, and go visit the intensive care ward for a while. Oops.

The second type of karma is what I call "modified" karma. This means that some lines of karma are still going to play out in the world, but due to awakening having occurred, these lines don't play out with the full force they would have had if the being they are playing through had not been awakened. You're on the same road, and you're still speeding, only you are clearer than you used to be, and you're starting to recognize that this is an unskillful pattern. So you slow down from 60 to 45 and only get a $100 traffic ticket for driving too fast for conditions.

The third type of karma is "negated" karma. You get in the car, but when your foot hits the pedal, it pushes the car to 35 instead of 60. You notice, "Wow, I'm driving much slower. I notice I feel calmer. I notice the neighbors do, too. Cool."

We typically notice negated karma by its absence rather than its presence. Conscious Awakeness has simply restructured the unit in some basic, beneficial ways. As J. Krishnamurti used to say about his headaches, "They're re-wiring me."

So this is the way Conscious Awakeness can affect a so-called individual's past karma going forward from vertical awakening. (Horizontal awakening includes all of the pre-awakening and post-awakening process. Vertical awakening refers to the event aspect, which most, but not all will experience.)

Of course karma is only something we can talk about in regard to the relative plane. Seen from the nondual view, there's no individual, and thus no karma is actually possible, but tell that to the cops when they're hauling you off to jail for something Mr. Doesn't Exist did some years back.

So what do you do when you're carrying a particularly heavy load from the past? Bring your helmet and skis, you're going for quite a ride. One of the reasons I couldn't quit drinking was that every time I quit I discovered that I was inheriting my own traumatized life. It felt like that life was such that anyone would have to drink over it, so it was back to the races.

Finally things got so bad that I had no choice. I wouldn't have quit drinking if I could have kept drinking, but I couldn't. I had shown a huge capacity for pain, but ultimately even I was surrendered. Being surrendered is when you tell yourself the truth: there's no way out. I couldn't drink successfully, and I couldn't quit trying to drink successfully.

This "I'm completely screwed and there's nothing I can do about it" moment is charmingly called surrender. But it's not something we do. It's something that happens automatically in response to truth. With the collapse of the ego, there is finally room for something new to come in, for the blind pattern to be broken, and for something fresh in the way of change to arise.

When that ton of bricks known as "acknowledged alcoholism" hit me, I stayed down. I stayed cooperative. In fact, I moved from cooperative to aggressively seeking change, and I was willing to go to any lengths to get it. I could smell a rat in the house, and he was wearing my shoes. I had been a creep and a criminal for much of my life.

So as I trod the boards of my karma's detritus, I took no shortcuts. If the only venue where I could still play was recovery, then I would at least be a winner there. I would out-spiritualize the competition and rise to the level of sainthood, which is when I hoped the women and money would start showing up.

But a funny thing happened as I was taking all this action. As I moved from intellectual spirituality to experiential spirituality, I actually changed. I became a whole new human, just like they'd told me you could. I never really believed it could happen to someone who'd been a homeless drunk and an utter ne'er do well, but it did anyway.

I was so happy that I figured my new halo and wings would be noticed by everybody. They weren't. People in recovery could see sweeping changes taking place, but people in my life saw the same guy with the same hair who walked the same way and talked with an unchanged accent. This points to the tremendous benefit and power of a healing community, like recovery.

People outside that community couldn't see that I was a new guy, and I get that. I'd been a "new guy" before and then fallen back in with the devil, so to speak. And let's recall that if I could have avoided becoming a new guy and just drunk myself to death, I would have done just that, so I'm not crowing for credit. But I really was completely changed by the action steps of recovery—somewhat against my egoic will.

Of course I still had some faults that were only slightly smaller than the one they call San Andreas, but the great news is that you can't see all that when you're making progress. Recovery's greatest line is, "We are not saints. We claim spiritual progress, not spiritual perfection."

When I took all that spiritual progress out into the world, I found a whole lot of closed doors. Prospective employers, banks, neighbors, and family were all looking at one thing: the ugly pumpkin that was the walking, talking testimony of my ruinous and ruined life.

I didn't get it. I was a very popular guy in recovery. People loved, respected, and trusted me. Finally I figured out why that was the case. In recovery, especially in early recovery, people were looking for and at the beautiful light that was shining through the ugly jack o'lantern. The rest of the world was still looking at the pumpkin.

Light will shine through any empty pumpkin you put it in, and I had become an empty pumpkin. And I was making a difference. I had gone from a homeless drunk to a contributing citizen. What a miracle! I can't tell you how big that was for me. So I let the "normies," as we sometimes called them, think what they wanted to think and did my own thing. They were going to think what they thought anyway, and there was no point in my suffering over it.

Six years after I sobered up, I woke up. I didn't earn it, unless you count suffering as earning, and if you do then I earned it many times over. No one earns awakening; it doesn't work anything at all like that. And the Light of Truth, just like the light of recovery, will shine through any old empty pumpkin it lands in. It has its own rules of efficiency, and it could not care less about ours. A flower will grow out of a littered Coca-Cola can or up through the cracks in a sidewalk. Birds will build a nest of trash. Life has no pride. It simply has a job to do, and it does it. It is beyond our opinions about it.

Now, I'm the first to agree, that I've got myself an ugly pumpkin. I cleaned it up as much as I could, but as I used to tell people in recovery, "If you start in a hole as deep as the one I started climbing out of, then it takes a long time just to get up to ground level." I didn't say that out of modesty. I wouldn't know modesty if it hit me in the face with a shovel. I said it out of accuracy. But I had a spade in my hand when I said it, and I was steadily filling up the terrible sinkhole that was my life.

After I woke up, I found out that I identified much more strongly with the nondual crowd than I did the recovery crowd. I stayed in recovery and basically translated nondual teaching into recovery speech, but there came a time when I simply had to declare loyalties, and I chose this path over that one. So when I started teaching openly, I once again let the "normies" think what they wanted to think. I was busy waking people up while wearing a police GPS monitor. It's a little incongruous, don't you think? Yet the people I worked with didn't give a damn about my monitor. They didn't give a damn about the ugly pumpkin. They were only interested in the Light. And they woke up.

When I got off of probation in 2011, I had already been teaching Nonduality in an informal fashion with the few interested people I could find in my vicinity, and I had been doing so for nearly a year. Once I was free to do as I pleased on the Internet, I started the original *Awakening Clarity*. I'd been restricted for a long time, and now I wanted to be involved.

A lot of people thought I was a nut. A good number of people have always thought I was a nut. Perhaps I am a nut. But I am a nut with a mission: I plan to live this life as happily and engaged as I can, regardless of its contents and conditions. Or, more properly, I plan to be as absent as I can so that Tao can live my life with the least amount of resistance possible.

So when I moved my teaching from my living room to the Internet, it never once occurred to me to get up there and announce what a shitty looking pumpkin I was. I talked about the Light that was shining through it. I figured that was what everyone wanted. I wrote and wrote and wrote, and my words never hurt anybody.

When I moved from just running the website to teaching via Skype, I have to tell you, once again it never for one second occurred to me to hang a shingle on my site pointing toward the ugly pumpkin. Hell, I'd already been doing having to do that for five years, and to a lesser degree I would have to live with that shingle around my neck for the rest of life—or until I don't, whichever comes first. Call me naïve or call me a con man, as some have, but I thought it was the present light that was the important part of spirituality. I still do.

Most of my clients work with me for about 2.5 hours, and I never see them again, or maybe I see them a couple of more times and then they're gone. Many of them drop me emails, but talking to me is not cheap, and the whole point of my teaching is not to create a dependency on me, it's to set people free. This teaching is not about so-called individuals. It's about an awakening Tao.

I simply don't believe that I owe these pass-through clients anything more than what they pay for: which is the greatest clarity that I can muster here (meaning the thinnest appearance of Fredness), so that I can hopefully help them muster that same clarity over there. I didn't choose to be a spiritual teacher. Spiritual teaching chose me. I'm doing the best I can, folks.

Granted, some of my clients use me as a clearing tool, and those who do, talk to me regularly. Some feel that my crowd should be shocked and dismayed at their choice of pumpkins, but the funny thing is they're not. My active, regular clients have been keenly supportive of me and this teaching, regardless. I have not lost a one.

A client in Germany, a publisher of nondual books in the German language, told me recently, "What you are teaching is the very nectar of Nonduality." I confess to having been really pleased by that. I realize I should be above all that, but I'm not.

I have no sangha, and I don't want one. I'm not even sure they're a great idea. Community, yes. Community based around a person? Not so much. I don't travel. I wouldn't live in an ashram with "a flock" at the point of a gun. I'm a married hermit and so is my wife. A big night for us is an hour of TV holding hands before she goes to sleep and I go read or write or meditate.

I do not see how this unit's karma has the slightest thing to do with anything else I do. For thousands of years in the West we have hung, burned, stoned, and crucified pumpkins for their pumpkin sins. And we get to busily ignore the light they carry when we do so, which is of course, the strategy. "Leave us in the dark. We can't see because we don't want to."

Here's a quote from a supportive email I got tonight from someone well-placed in the nondual community. "Your particular situation makes very little sense to me. The whole point of this is that it is all about transformation. You would think that people would see you as a poster child for that. I can't understand the harsh feelings for something that happened so long ago, and pre-transformation, either."

We point outward so that we don't have to look inward. It's popular, but I'm not sure it's productive. We are, in effect, calling God on the carpet, correcting her errors of judgment in her timing and placement of lights, and telling her how things should be. Because we are the ultimate benchmarks of the world, and we know.

I have a job to do. I'm to wake people up until I don't. I didn't cause that, and I can't stop it. I don't think criticism can either. From homeless drunk to contributing citizen. Wow. I don't think I'm everyone's teacher, nor do I ever imply that. In recovery I used to tell freshly sobering drunks, "The bad news is that you've got to be pretty damn sick if I'm going to be the doctor. The good news is, you qualify!"

That same thing applies in Nonduality. I may not be much of a pumpkin, but to the people who are tired, scared, confused, lonely, suffering, and paying more attention to the Light than the jack o'lantern, I seem to be reasonably helpful. So, if you want a lily white teacher, keep on shopping. If you're willing to work with recycled material, welcome aboard.

QUESTIONING THE ULTIMATE AUTHORITY

Do we still have, as Suzuki Roshi aptly called it, Beginner's Mind? Or are we in the middle of the pack and the middle of the muck? Are we still pushing upward and outward, or have we relaxed and found that place of comfort? Have we traded liberation for stagnation? Do we know so much now that we've forgotten that the key is not found in what we know but in what we are willing to unknow?

I've talked with people—and woken them up—who've been seeking the Magic Practice, or the Magic Tip, or the Magic Teacher and/or Tradition for forty years and even more. Some would say they're holding out for The Miracle, and a few—a very few—would be right: they'll get it. My sense is a little more pragmatic. I'd say that most of them are simply barking up the wrong tree.

Every time someone wakes up, it's something of a miracle, I grant you that. So is electricity, but it powers the lights in my study almost every single time I hit the switch. If the light doesn't come on, then there's something wrong with either the wiring or something else out in the field. You can bet that electricity itself is never found be functioning improperly. Same thing in what we're doing. Awakeness is always working, and it's always working perfectly.

In the early twenty-first century, awakening is becoming an everyday miracle. I can't know what was possible a thousand years ago, or a hundred years ago, or even twenty. But I know very well what's available now—and not just at my house. If you want to wake up, you can. Now here's the toughest question: Do you really, really want to?

Many folks will say "yes" to that question, but a lot of them are not telling the truth, I can promise you that. Over time we may trade in our dream of liberation for the reality of community and comfort. That's one way to stagnate, but not the only one by any stretch.

Once in a while I find people who say they want to wake up, but what they really mean is, "I want to wake up on my terms." Not gonna happen. In the first place, the one who's holding these terms is the very reason their terms are not being met. Most or all of us have expectations in regard to awakening—certainly I did. I held onto those terms until the vise of suffering became too much to bear. Then I unwittingly dropped all demands, and guess what? That's just when awakening happened—after I let go. Specifically, I had been holding out for a fireworks type of awakening. I wanted all the LSD effects I could get. After all, I'd thoroughly enjoyed LSD back in the day.

Yes, I wanted the Addict's Jolt, but I was also holding out for an awakening that would fix all of my relative problems. I had no shortage of them, let me tell you. And when they got painful enough, I finally lost all interest in the Fred story. Who wants to suffer in a nightmare? Not me.

When I finally threw in the towel on Fred, I threw it all in—Fred's advice, Fred's wisdom, Fred's lies, Fred's fantasies, Fred's life management skills, Fred's reputation, his imagined dignity—I just didn't give a damn about him. And awakening happened. I didn't do it, I just didn't get in the way of it.

People regularly ask me how to surrender, and as I regularly point out, you already do it twice a day. You do it first when you wake up in the morning, and then again when you go to sleep at night. How do you do that? You don't. You become willing for it to happen, and then it happens by itself. Surrender of the self is no different.

Not all of us, thank God, are going to have the sort of painful life content that I did. I do notice, however, that a number of teachers in our community had similar experiences to mine, where suffering was key, so my case is by no means an anomaly. My spiritual tradition was essentially Worship of Fredness. That's what I wasn't questioning. When I became willing to question it—no, "revoke it" is a better phrase—the game changed.

Fredness was my ultimate authority. Fredness, for God's sake, was my spiritual teacher. Fredness was my God.

In those days I was a Bookstore Buddhism guy—that's my lineage. I would've been a Bookstore Advaita guy, except that I'd never heard of it, and I was sure that Buddhism in general and specifically Zen, was the one true path. I wouldn't listen to any teacher who didn't preach the gospel of meditation, which unfortunately left out a few very good ones—like J. Krishnamurti.

In my opinion, which was the only opinion I put any stock in, other religions and traditions simply had it wrong. Other religions had a God, for goodness sake. I, on the other hand, had No-God, which was simply the same god the other traditions had, only my No-God wore a hat and sunglasses like some reclusive movie star, so I didn't have to confront her head-on. She didn't embarrass me in public.

Bookstore Buddhism was the only game my ego would let me play; I wasn't a joiner of communities —unless of course, you wanted to make me the leader. I'm by no means alone in this Bookstore Lineage; a great many of us come from it. We have our own set of historical, celebrity teachers. Our robe is usually the bathrobe and our ashram has a two-car attached garage.

I'm not saying self-leadership is a bad thing—necessity is the mother of invention. But I think you're going to have to be as lucky as a leprechaun to have much in the way of long-term success with it. It gets tougher and tougher for the ego to get rid of the ego. In my case, however, it left me with a damn fool of teacher and a damn fool of a student. This was the case for me not only prior to awakening, but for three-and-a-half years after awakening as well.

Eventually I gave up on my teacher. Fredness was seen to be shallow and narrow and a liar to boot. You don't have to give up on your teacher, whether it's you or someone else, no matter what lineage you're in—unless, of course, you do. Lightning can strike on a clear day, but I wouldn't bet on it hitting me. Yet that's precisely what I was betting on for years—decades. I was betting on a long shot. I just couldn't tell myself the truth about my own tradition of no-tradition or about my unwise, unscrupulous teacher.

I loved Fredness way too much to be honest about him, and I loved his Holy Way. I worshiped him and his Holy Way on Mondays, Wednesdays, and Fridays, yet I loathed him and his No-Way-Out on the other four days. People often tell me they feel the same way about their own spiritual path, whether it's organized to the point of being anal or disorganized to the point of being chaotic, as mine was. On a very regular basis—every week—people tell me they are tired of being tired; they are sick and tired of reading nothing but spiritual books, but they find they're unable to read anything else. It seems that oftentimes our path exists simply to wear us out, which creates an opening for liberation, but the path itself will never actually deliver us from itself.

A client recently said, "I'm a yoga teacher and have been doing yoga for twenty-five years. Yoga was my spiritual practice. I was (and still am) devoted to it. But when you asked 'Has your spiritual path become a dead end?' I immediately saw that yoga had in fact become a dead end for me spiritually. It was comfortable, and I don't know that spirituality is supposed to be especially comfortable."

I respect this open, honest attitude so much. This client was willing to question her path and her progress. And as a result she woke up extremely clearly. We hear a great deal about being our own authority in Nonduality, but have we turned this advice into a detriment? Have we become overconfident or simply lazy? Do we find ourselves waiting for the Universe to make the first move but not really expecting it to?

So, what's your ultimate authority? Is it your teacher? Your tradition? Your library? Is it your "renegade" path that smacks so heavily of all the other "renegade" paths?

Of course, in the end your ultimate authority is always you, but be willing to look at your own situation in the same logical-yet-compassionate way that you would address your best friend's situation if he or she asked you to. If what you're doing is working for you, great, have at it. My hat is off. After all, I can't even know what this unit should do until it does it, so I'm no authority on what's right for anyone else. Nonetheless, I do have a couple of suggestions.

If your present path is not working for you but it's working for others, retreat at least temporarily and reassess. If it's not working for you or much of anyone else, get the hell out there and try something else. Life's too short.

THE VISE OF SUFFERING

Like most of the other work in this book, this piece began as a post for my website *Awakening Clarity Now*. I worked on it for over a week and stayed up past 1:00 a.m. one night to finish it, only when I hit "Publish," I got an error code. I clicked again, and the last two hours of my writing disappeared into the ether, even though it had theoretically been saved. Ugh. As you might imagine, this event did not fall within the unit's preferences. It was not a happy unit for a little while.

So I took my broken heart and went elsewhere for a few days, working on other things, including actually sitting down to read and meditate at some length. My wound began to heal, and I thought again about finishing that lost post. But not quite yet.

And then, after cutting a video on Deep Attention Practice, I somewhat grudgingly went back to work on the piece that had disappeared. The funny thing is, as Nature would have it, this new post is a whole lot better than was the phantom one. It's twice as long, twice as deep, and reads better, too. That's not so surprising because, even while my gut was still reeling from that into-the-ether punch, it had occurred to me that I wasn't "supposed" to have published the post in that form, which is absolutely true. However, at the moment of loss, I was not yet ready to fully accept that wisdom because I had a warm and cuddly victim story that I wanted to nurse for a little while.

These units really do want things to go their way, and I notice that my unit, Fredness, is not yet an exception to that longing. I don't think I'll hold my breath until that happens. For now I can notice such nonsense and remember not to take it seriously. Nature had apparently just benevolently saved me from publishing a post-that-should-not-be. Great. Thank you, damn it. So, here is the one that obviously was meant to be.

Gary Falk is a very long-term, well-known member of our

spiritual community. There is very little in the way of "what you can do" to find enlightenment that Gary hasn't done. You don't find many people who've been on the narrow path of Nonduality for 45 years, but Gary is one of them. He will tell you himself that it's been a hard rocky road that's wound around gurus, cults, religions, teachers, workshops galore, and who knows what all else. He has experienced pretty much everything available except awakening.

I first came into contact with Gary when I got an email from him a few weeks back asking for information about sessions. He was especially interested in the amount of time between sessions, since he considered himself something of a "lazy seeker" and didn't want to feel rushed. That cracked me up. You don't stay on the path for more than four decades if you're lazy. No way. A lazy man would've long since shot himself in the name of efficiency.

Gary told me that he'd tried to "call off the search" any number of times only to discover that he doesn't have the power to call off the search. It's not his decision to make. Amen, brother—been there, done that, got the t-shirt. We don't choose to be seekers; seeking chooses us, whether we like it or not. And then it makes of us what it will.

I can remember quite well when I would have been more than willing to trade in all of my spiritual books, practices, accoutrements, and knowledge, if I could just for once, be a normal automaton of a guy drinking beer and watching football at Hooter's. For a guy in the kind of mental turmoil I was in, that scene looked better than an ad for a vacation in Fiji. Spiritual-smiritual—who needs it?

Back to Gary and his quandary. In a funny but not completely inaccurate way, you could say that I've never left my old Twelve Step recovery position of "sponsor." Only these days I work with seekaholics, instead of alcoholics. It's the same disease manifesting in two different ways and with the same defense mechanism: denial. Seekaholics are addicted to separation while simultaneously experiencing a desperate craving to give it up. Ugh. I remember that sensation so well, as both a seekaholic and an alcoholic. Instead of always being on the prowl for their next drink, however, seekaholics are always looking for their next think.

Just by following the simple, seemingly harmless, thought, "It's okay if I go have one drink..." or "It's okay if I go have just one think..." either addict (or the same addict suffering from both conditions) can go on a sudden bender that ends up lasting for years. I don't know for sure that seekaholism will actually land you in the gutter—although I can say for certain that it aided and abetted my trips there. On the other hand, I don't   believe you will get arrested for driving under the influence of too many pointers, but it's still a rough ride, no matter your vehicle. "Hey, buddy, could you spare a guy an opinion?"

I'm overdoing it here in the name of humor. Thought is not our enemy. Ego is not our enemy. Desire is not our enemy. In fact, we don't even have an enemy. But we do have some tricky friends.

At any rate, I sent Gary some information, and we scheduled five appointments. I found that he was living with his 100-year-old mother on Staten Island. When we met for our Introductory Session, I was thoroughly charmed and laughing like crazy a lot of the time. Gary was all New Yorker: loud and animated, completely up-front and unabashed, as well as being a very funny guy. From time to time he would be looking at me and laughing while loudly talking to his mother, who was pleasantly wandering about the apartment.

It was a stitch. And we got along quite wonderfully. That's not unusual for me, but the level of connection we had was delightfully keen.

After a few minutes of talk, it became apparent that after so many decades on the enlightenment trail, Gary knew a lot. A whole lot. The language of Nonduality slipped from his lips as easily as it did from mine. I knew immediately that the challenge with Gary was going to be the fact that he might know too much. This is common. It must be overcome if the client is to awaken.

The reader will note that I am the author of a little volume entitled   *The Book of Unknowing*, and it should be clear from the title that it's not my sense that enlightenment is contingent upon getting more information. I do just the opposite. I help folks un-know what they already know. And I could see I had my work cut out for me with this guy. I usually do. In fact, Gary is more like a composite client, meaning that he is positively the norm and not the exception.

"You know, Gary," I said, "all of this time you've spent on the path may not be working for you. I'm afraid it may very well be working against you." Gary readily agreed. He could see the truth of that, and he knew it before he talked to me; he just didn't know what to do about it. Perfect! That's right where I need a client to be, and his easy agreement on that point was a real plus.

To start with, I helped Gary see that if just words and practices hadn't freed him by now then it was increasingly unlikely that they ever would. I helped him see that if the last four decades of trying it his way hadn't worked, then the odds were bad that another two hours of doing more of the same was going to be the magic bullet. Could he go ahead and allow himself to fail? Could he hand himself over to experience and not theory? Was he willing to put his attention on the evidence of his actual experience instead of his thoughts about his experience.

I walked him through the hopeless nature of his condition, which is not unlike the condition of most of us, though perhaps he had spent a bit longer in that unfulfilled state. Gary's seeking had led him on a dry and often discouraging search. Endless books and workshops. Endless CDs and DVDs. Endless teachers and talks with teachers. And still not consciously awake. Maybe a glimpse and maybe not. It seems we absolutely can't wake up and we absolutely can't quit trying to wake up. Modification doesn't work. Control doesn't work. Sincerely pretending to give up control doesn't work. At some point, if we are lucky, we run fresh out of ideas.

When we clearly realize that we can't successfully do something while simultaneously clearly realizing that we can't successfully quit trying to do it, then we have walked right into the awful yet wonderful Vise of Suffering. Imagine a steel room with no doors, no windows, absolutely no way out. And then two of the walls start moving toward you. At first you scramble around looking for a secret door, a button, anything, any way out at all. Finding none, you holler for help at the top of your lungs. As the walls get close, you put your arms out and try to stop them. No dice.

In this slowly constricting room, there will come a point when it's seen and known that This Is It. End of story. It's not about right or wrong, fair or unfair, being too early or being too late. Things are as they are and death is coming for this unit in just moments. No way out. Once this was clear, then I think for many of us, perhaps even for most of us, panic would finally yield to peace. There is nothing left to fight and no fight left in us. The candle is being blown out.

And in our surrender we are crushed.

Ultimately surrender only seems like something we do. In truth it's something that happens. It's a spontaneous, internal shift that automatically occurs when we accept and acknowledge the utter truth of our powerlessness. Far more than mere resignation is required. Resignation is just resistance in a nice hat. Surrender is agreeing to cooperate with the inevitable.

The Vise of Suffering opens only as widely and speedily as we do. It's not a matter of giving up the reins *or* perishing, it's more a matter of giving up the reins *and* perishing, all within that same movement, within that same moment. I would never wish this thing on anybody, but I do notice it works to awaken us more effectively and more often than any other motivation I've yet seen. There's nothing quite like a boiling combination of fear, pain, suffering, and surrender to generate change. It worked for me.

I saw that Gary had come to a similar point. Instead of wanting to win a nondual knowledge contest, Gary sounded to me like he really wanted to wake up. We can appear to win almost any argument with any sage, because ultimately they won't resist your argument. They will neither confirm nor deny. They will just shut up and let you carry on your insanity without their help. You get to win—which in this case means that you have successfully thwarted awakening.

I can't stress enough how critical Gary's clear seeing and easy acknowledgment of his current, clueless condition were in facilitating an awakening event. For awakening to occur, It must be seen that the me who's trying to do it simply can't. Ultimately, that me is its own anti-catalyst. If awakening does ever happen, you can bet your bottom dollar that it's not going to happen to that unit. Openness and willingness are everything.

What I found in Gary was a well-disguised but nevertheless golden combination of honesty and humility. And guess what? He woke up. Very clearly. He has tremendous context, and since nothing is ever wasted, he not only woke up more clearly than many but also is likely to clear up more quickly as well, not that there's a race going on or any eventual graduation day. It all happens as it happens, and in Gary's case, the Vise of Suffering chalked up another win.

SO WHAT?

Sadly enough, all too often the nondual path seems to be a movement from innocent enthusiasm to jaded skepticism or even bitterness. Heads up: If that's your experience, you're doing it wrong.

The idea that we can sit on the sidelines in our bathrobes and just watch others play the "spiritual game" and expect to have clarity delivered to us via room service is both foolish and flawed. I have met a broad swath of people in the nondual spiritual community and the ones I notice are waking up and clearing up are the people who do something. They are ahead by a mile.

Please don't talk to me about "no doer." Been there, done that, got the t-shirt. It didn't work for me, and the odds are really really high that it's not going to work for you either. Praying for a bolt of lightning is not nearly so effective as walking through the storm with a long metal pole on your shoulder. Do something.

It's completely paradoxical. I'm the first to agree that on the surface it makes no sense whatsoever, but from what I have seen in the hundreds of awakenings I've played a part in, we absolutely positively can either markedly encourage or discourage Conscious Awakeness to begin to flow through a given unit.

My observations tell me that if we're not deeply actively involved in making every effort to wake up, then it's probably not going to happen for us. It's time to grow up and, regardless of paradox and rumor, take a little responsibility for our own awakenings. Forget all the philosophical hoodoo about "who it would be that could do that, because I know I don't really exist." If you are not consciously awake to your True Nature right this minute, then the odds are stacked to the sky that you do think you exist as a unit and that you think you are that unit—the one who's reading these words.

So instead of living in nondual denial as a result of what you have read and think and want to believe, take advantage of that situation and use the unit to help you. Don't try to understand it, do it. So long as it feels like there's someone there who can take action and make decisions, then I strongly advise you to do so.

The people who, in the main, are waking up and clearing up are those who have been honest and humble enough to see through the very limited and limiting "there's nothing to do, and no one to do it" and have made an active commitment to their own spiritual well-being and so-called advancement. Have you? Have you really?

Nisargadatta called this quality earnestness; I call it willingness. He and I are talking about the same thing, and like me, percentage-wise he did not see all that much of it. It forever amazed him, and it amazes me. There is such a sense of entitlement out there now. We have been so overwhelmed by the amount of previously-precious-now-yawner material presented to us daily via the Internet that in many cases we no longer bother to vet it, respect it, or support it. We have some notion that "everyone should be supporting me and my awakening" even though I'm not doing anything myself.

I don't mind sharing with a straight face that in my seeking days I was consumed by awakening. I read and listened to everything I could get my hands on. I wrote bloggers and authors. I worked in the background for years writing book reviews to support writers, publishers, and other seekers. Finally I started the original *Awakening Clarity* blog where again I actively promoted that same crowd. I hung links for blogs and teachers, directing traffic to their websites. I got involved.

And you know what? I woke up and cleared up. The spiritual path is essentially the movement from "What can I get?" to "How can I help?" I had been a taker all of my life, but I finally learned the way the world really works, and I began to play by those rules. The rest of the story is self-evident.

I am leveling with you friend-to friend, person-to-person, not as some lofty spiritual teacher who lives on a cloud. I am one of you guys, an average-Joe spiritual seeker who rode the roller coaster of disappointment, depression, and desperation, and finally had the amazing experience of having Conscious Awakeness begin to flow through this husk; nothing more, nothing less. Do as you will, but don't say I didn't point you in the right direction.

THE POWER OF COMMITMENT

The transfer of our identification from the illusion of personhood to the truth of unity is a difficult one. Even though we may project that there was little difficulty for this teacher or that saint, the odds are extremely high that we have either been misinformed or we have misinterpreted what really happened in that case. I can't know what is or is not possible, but I can tell you that of the hundreds of people I know who have awakened both with me and without me, not a single one of them had a cakewalk either before or after awakening. In most cases, which will almost surely include your own, it just doesn't work that way.

Every week I have Awakening Sessions with people who tell me at the beginning of our session that they no longer seriously identify with the unit, only to discover thirty minutes later that in fact they do. One is an intellectual understanding, which I am in no way underrating, and the other is a felt knowing. There's quite a difference. Even people who are awake when we meet will almost always discover pockets of residual identification when we do a thorough investigation.

By pockets of residual identification I don't mean the biologically essential relationship we have with our bodies. Without that relationship the unit cannot remain alive, so that's not going anywhere. I still know what part of my body to feed and where to put a jacket when it's cold, and so did St. Francis and Ramana Maharshi. I will turn around if you call the unit's name, and they would have done the same if you called theirs.

So what we are talking about is psychological identification, where we think ourselves to be our minds. As addictive as the body can be, it doesn't compare to the cravings of the mind. And, in the final analysis, regardless of the excellent teaching strategies that we hear state otherwise, ultimately we actually are our bodies, we are simply not limited to being our bodies. Like everything else we are ever taught, "I am not the body" is a statement about a stage within ever-unfolding clarity, not an absolute truth.

Just as we use one thorn to dig out another, pointers are helpful little white lies to move us beyond them. Use them and lose them.

A legendary Zen koan states:

"First, mountains were mountains and rivers were rivers." (Pre-enlightenment.)

"Next, mountains were no longer mountains, and rivers were no longer rivers." (Early enlightenment.)

"Finally, mountains are mountains and rivers are rivers." (Mature enlightenment.)

If you'll forgive the awkwardness of the phrase, "we are Oneness." Given this, we can't be Oneness and somehow exclude our bodies. Nonduality is always inclusive, never exclusive. We can declare that our bodies, these physical units, are for all practical purposes "real." What I mean by "real" in this instance is that these bodies remain present whether we are or are not thinking about them. Contrarily, the apparent existence of the characters we play is reliant upon present thought.

The character can be found in experience, but it is not located in reality. Experience is enough—it's okay to enjoy experiences and take them relatively seriously, but ultimately only so seriously. Parents filling a stocking for a small child are taking Santa Claus seriously, but they don't believe in Santa Claus. They have gone shopping beforehand; they are not waiting to hear reindeer on the roof.

It is the nagging, almost overwhelming belief in the character's existence that confuses us. It is this belief that draws the line between unconscious awakeness and Conscious Awakeness. The Fred story was hugely detailed, and I had an enormous investment in it. It ran every morning, matinee, and evening for over fifty years. It had patterns within patterns within patterns. And some of those patterns are still running.

The character is, in effect, a meta-pattern. The philosophical truth that "it doesn't exist" holds up quite poorly in the face of the living breathing fact that it sure appears to. We refer to it, and we defer to it constantly. And it is to this pattern that we turn to for help in waking up.

I doubt I need to hammer home the point that a pattern can't wake up a pattern from nearly eternal pattern-ness. This is completely and ridiculously obvious once it's seen, but it can't even be guessed at when it's not. It is as well-disguised and tricky as the cosmic joke of awakening itself—whose punch line is also glaringly obvious, but only when seen in a rear-view mirror.

The automated patterns that we successively think we are, can and do go through countless lifetimes trying to wake themselves up. And that's fine—it's their job to do that. Until it isn't. How can we know when "isn't" has arrived? We will find ourselves on either an overt or a covert spiritual path.

A really sure sign that you, the Reader, are fast running out of story-time in this four dimensional DNA-driven dream, a totally unmistakable sign, is the fact that you just read this paragraph. When it's time to get obvious, the pull to Conscious Awakeness won't hesitate to smack us squarely in the forehead. Smack.

This idea might be a real comfort for us, if it meant anything in a human-relative sense. It doesn't. Given that we are talking about hundreds or thousands of lifetimes per dream-line, then to be a paltry five hundred or a thousand years from waking up would be considered really close. I'm not actually suggesting that spiritual development is measured by a given number of Earth-orbits around the random star we call "the sun," but such an idea can make this slippery concept slightly less slippery. Use it and lose it.

Everyone will wake up in the end; that's how it works. There's really nothing to it. Unless there is. This time around for me, childhood physical and mental abuse, alcoholism and fill-in-the-blank addiction, homelessness, loss of family, health, and dignity, along with two longish trips to a mental hospital and about thirty trips to jail turned the trick very nicely. Suffering is a bummer of a path, but it's a sure one. And one has to say that I was surely committed to it.

But of course this is not the kind of commitment I'm talking about. What I'm speaking of here is conscious commitment— making the decision over and over again—to do whatever it takes to wake up; to step up to the plate again and again and swing as hard as you can and damn the scoreboard. That type of commitment includes taking stock of where you are right now. We have to be willing to tell ourselves the truth today, and today, and today.

I had a session with a guy out in California's beautiful canyon country this past week. As most of my clients are, he was a very smart, and as is also common, he was quite a long-term, experienced member of our community. He told me he went to sleep in the middle of the fourth grade, and that he'd been trying to wake up ever since—meaning for the last thirty or forty years. He said he'd been in cults, religions, movements, what have you. He'd had lots of teachers East and West, including some powerful ones. His use of Nondualese was as fluid and fluent as my own.

He was a totally committed guy. This was not only evident from the path he'd been walking for all of these decades: he proved to me that he was totally committed right then, that day, in that very moment. How did he prove it? Like this.

Two minutes into our intro he stopped talking, looked me squarely in the eye, and without hesitation said, "I think I talk above my realization. I think I need some remedial help." It blew me away. My respect for this guy shot through the roof immediately, and I told him so. I should be hearing this kind of confession on an almost daily basis. I don't.

This is someone who was ready to shed whatever he thought he knew—and whoever he thought he was—in the service of Truth. This was a guy who could see that whatever he'd been doing, no matter how good and skillful it might be for others, wasn't actually working for him to the degree necessary to foster Self-realization. He was an empty cup ready to accept whatever I was about to pour. Beautiful.

The most valuable thing any of us can ever know is that we don't know anything. That doesn't mean denying or tossing away all of our relative and relevant knowledge structure. It just means opening up the hatch and hurling sureness overboard. Doubt is our friend.

Less than an hour into our inquiry, my new friend came to a shattering realization of what he was not. It's a simple but staggering insight into the mechanism of the dream. His world changed right there. He saw it so clearly that reviewing what he Is was almost rote, as he meandered through a list of gentle stories and reminders to That which had just experienced Truth about what It already knew. That could have never happened without the humility this guy displayed up front; he'd been his own best friend.

If you've been in a tradition for a long time, and you haven't woken up yet, ask yourself why you're still there. Are you yet seeking enlightenment, or are you perhaps hanging onto the known, the comfortable beliefs, rituals, practices, and community? There's nothing wrong with the latter, just be honest with yourself about it—you'll enjoy it more, and the pressure will be off for you to be anything other than what you already are—which is all you can be anyway.

If you are digging a bunch of shallow holes looking for water—trying this, then that; now this teacher, then that one—once again, ask yourself why. Are you sincere in your quest, or are you having a good time eating appetizers without having to commit to an entrée? Again, there's nothing wrong with that, but don't lie to yourself about it. Acknowledge that you're a dilettante and be willing to settle for a dilettante's rewards.

If enlightenment is right around the same damn corner it was two, or five, or fifty years ago, and you genuinely want to wake up, then commit—right now! Commit to doing whatever it takes to wake up and you will wake up. Period.

And then commit again. Do whatever it takes to clear up—to abide, to endure, to embody—to be awake to this arising, the only arising that actually counts. Good luck. Let me know if I can help.

THE NONDUAL RELATIONSHIP

It takes exactly one person to have a great relationship. While this article is going to generally focus on the romantic relationship, the same general rules apply to all types. After all, in the final analysis, there's only one thing going on here, and you happen to be that one thing. This very arising—this one—is how you are expressing yourself to yourself at this so-called moment. You are the whole thing, the everything—including the no-thing from which all of this magically springs forth. There's no such thing as oneness plus or oneness minus.

Nothing you can see, hear, feel, taste, touch, or think is other than you. The sum total of manifestation does not equal you, but it is not other than you. In this so-called moment I, as a writer, am currently creating an article to myself as a reader, with myself as a computer, while sitting within myself as an apartment, and on and on ad infinitum. When we say that there is no separation, this refers not merely to the unity of space but to the unity of time as well, so "my" writing and "your" reading, despite appearances, are taking place simultaneously.

There is only Here and Now and even those words are only indicating different expressions of the one thing going on. It is more accurate to say there is only Here/Now, this single, undulating world consisting of an endless chain of multiple appearances.

The natural response of Awakeness, upon its realization of its living wholeness, is love, acceptance, and generosity. Any other movement is likely to be egoic. The authentic response is to give, not to take. What can Conscious Awakeness possibly need, given that it already has everything?

When we expect others to take care of our needs, we're already in separation. Granted, we are talking about oneness, not sameness, so at one level or another there is the feel of "I" and "other." Yet even if we have not had a radical awakening, if we are willing to hold the truth of unity in our hearts and heads and act on it within the world, a whole other level of relationship becomes available.

In fact, a whole new world will become available. It's already here. Absolute peace and absolute harmony are always available. They are what's underlying the ever-changing appearances of chaos. We will experience whichever one we put our attention on, immediately upon putting our focus on it.

Whatever we put our attention upon expands within our experience. Whatever we withdraw our attention from will contract within our experience. Everyone reading this article is awakening. When we begin to act upon whatever level of clarity we currently have, that is actually clarity in action in Here/Now.

We get what we need when we need it, but not before. When we utilize what we've already been granted, that's emptying the proverbial teacup and opening up room for more. That process is known as flow. All too often we act like the Dead Sea, which has no outlet and will support no life.

Giving is the key. Allowing is the key. Loving first is the key.

There is nothing but relationship. Nothing stands alone. Everything supports everything else. As individuals we are neither negligible nor special. We are, in an individual sense, part of. We are, in a universal sense, all of.

If we want a great relationship—whether it's with our romantic partner, our parents, children, PTA, or anyone else— what is required is that we act from the ground of unity and remain completely open about when, how, and if others do what we see as their part. Their requirement is to be themselves. After all, that's who we love, is it not?

If we find that we are in love with a dream-to-be, if we are betting-on-the-come, we are going to be miserable. Always. Our family, friends, and community are who they are. They are not who we want them to be unless we want them as they are. Any stipulation we put forward is the first act of incompatibility.

If we find that we are in a relationship that for some reason is no longer working for us, whether it's with a partner or a business, we owe it to ourselves and to everyone else to do one of three things: fix it, surrender to it, or get out of it. It is neither helpful nor skillful to allow things to run on unchanged with everyone suffering when all we're doing about it is complaining. Sometimes love means saying you're sorry, and sometimes love means saying goodbye. Do what feels true and don't look back. And this, too, can be a great relationship.

Generally speaking, we have to choose between our love for our partners and our love of our expectations. If the former wins out, then it means the dropping of the second. All conditions are out.

Let me share a bit about the relationship I have with my wife, Betsy. I'm not setting this up to be some arbitrary standard, I'm simply sharing my personal experience. I think it's important to share what's available for those of us on this path.

Betsy and I met thirteen years ago via Twelve Step recovery. After a bit of initial adjustment, it was clear that "we were a deal." I remember quite vividly a weekend we spent together in the mountains a couple of months after we got together. In my egoic idiocy, I had always been a guy who tried to change my wives and girlfriends to suit my taste.

On this mountain trip, Betsy, who at that that time was far saner than I was, said, "Let's work to help each other get well." We hugged and when we did, a voice spoke up in my head as clearly as if from someone in the room with us. That voice gave me what may be the greatest advice I ever took. It said simply, "Don't try to change this one. She's perfect the way she is."

Crazy as I still was at 18 months sober, that voice nonetheless made a huge impression on me. And to this day, I have tried to live up to that standard and have done pretty well. Betsy does the same with me. Being allowed to be who you are anyway is a great relief, and it takes a lot of pressure off of both partners.

I don't think Betsy heard a voice on that trip, because she didn't need to. She already knew. In her mind she already had a perfect diamond—it was simply still in the rough! She did not set about trying to change me into the man of her dreams; rather, she set about trying to help me grow into someone it was worth her dreaming about. I can't tell begin to tell you how much foresight that took!

Initially I was drawn to Betsy because she had a sense of presence I had never felt before. Then she spoke in a meeting one day about spending a Saturday afternoon with her dogs, cat, a bagel, a book, and a nap. I was toast. The scene she had described played over and over in my head. There was an almost mystical aura around it. This was what I wanted to appear in my life, and I resolved to go after it.

I had to be a bit patient at first, which I have never been any good at. But I was only a few months sober, and like Groucho Marx not wanting to belong to any club that would have him as a member, I felt the same way about Betsy. I wanted to get healthier before I approached her with any agenda beyond being cordial at meeting time.

I wasn't the only one who could feel Betsy's impact—virtually everyone in our recovery community could. Everybody loved her. She could read the steps or promises out loud and every person in the room could feel their hearts shift. There was something about her.

I now know that what I was feeling was latent Awakeness. Betsy was on the cusp of awakening for years, long before her drinking and into early recovery. With my flowering would come the words that actualized Betsy's latency into Conscious Awakeness.

Betsy had no overt spiritual pull and certainly no spiritual language. Her path was that of beauty. As she made her way through life, the physical environment in her wake sprang into breathtaking loveliness, as if she were some combination of an interior decorator and Johnny Appleseed. We need people like that, and more than you might think.

The other notable thing about Betsy is that she was (and is) incredibly grateful and innately generous. And she was a master at handling a rough cob like me. Not manipulating—handling.

I was a chain smoker and Betsy was a non-smoker. That's trouble, it just is. Betsy never once asked me to quit or even suggested it. She would look at me with bright eyes and a smile and say, "You don't look like a smoker to me. You won't smoke forever, I'm sure of it."

No nagging, no pressure, just loving encouragement. Had she handled it any other way, my ego would have felt forced to resist her, just to prove its independence. As it was, I was keen to cooperate. And eventually I did cooperate. Two-and-half years after we started dating I quit smoking, an act so radical that it shocked my friends. They could believe I quit drinking, but no one could believe I actually quit smoking. After all, I had been a very serious smoker. Only half in jest I would say, "You know, this damn breathing is interfering with my smoking!"

Giving up cigarettes was an extremely difficult thing for me to do. I can remember sitting in a pizza joint with Betsy holding my hand as tears streamed down my cheeks because I wanted to smoke so badly. I quit for love. I wanted to give Betsy a smoke-free boyfriend more than I wanted to take another drag on a cigarette. She got her gift, and I got rid of what I saw as a threat to our future together.

We are like the two hands of a clock, always pulling together, always moving in the same direction, always with a common goal—happiness, safety, and security for our little multiple-species family. If ever wife and husband were yin and yang, we are.

We eat out several times a week, but when we eat at home, here is how mealtime works for us. Unless I am in session or otherwise indisposed, I set the table. Betsy cooks. Every dinner is a music-and-candles event. Then I wash the dishes. The next morning Betsy puts the dry dishes away. We have never once had a discussion about any of this. It has simply unfolded this way.

Betsy pays dog bills, and I pay cat bills. If some vet bill or other surprise bill is particularly onerous, the other will reach across the table and help out. There is no you, no me, only us. All of this happens naturally as we each strive to move in a way that best accommodates and fulfills the other. It's not a strategy, it's simply a way of life. In the last thirteen years we have become almost literally a singular, seamless whole.

Sex is a big deal in romantic relationships, and happily we have been sexually compatible since the beginning. Having both been practicing alcoholics for decades, our partnership inherited some strange history, and sexual baggage was part of that. We were always candid about our pasts, and none of it has ever been a problem for either of us. That was then, and this is now, and now is all that counts, because now is all that is.

As a loving couple we've certainly talked about our sex lives any number of times over the years, always in a bid to keep communication in that area frank and strong. Almost since the beginning our own desires have been entirely secondary to what the other one wants or needs. It's amazing how generous that attitude can make your partner feel. It's not a strategy, but it's worth noticing.

In fact, it's fair to say that we talk about everything. Nothing is off the table, and we talk in some depth, at least briefly, every day. Betsy is my third wife, and all three wives have been card-carrying geniuses. Even as a young man I could see that I could talk a whole lot longer than I could make love, and I wanted to make sure I was in interesting company.

Initially there was that wonderful sense of compelling urgency. For a lot of years we had a regular Wednesday night "appointment," followed by Date Night. Wednesday nights are still Date Nights at our house—we still dress up a bit and eat out together, but these days we may or may not have started the evening upstairs. It's all good either way.

Another hot button in relationships, of course, is money. When Betsy met me I was as poor as a rat. Though she didn't have a lot, she had a hell of a lot more than I did. And she had an endless attic. Almost every time she came to see me she brought me some household item until I had a lovely little apartment even though most of the time I didn't have two dimes to rub together.

For the first ten years of our relationship, Betsy earned significantly more than I did. She never cared about that, and if she didn't, I didn't . My ego was perfectly willing to accept a bit of bruising if it meant that due to her largess we could eat pizza in a restaurant on a Saturday night.

Interestingly enough, some time ago that trend reversed itself, and suddenly I became the foremost breadwinner. Nothing changed; we never skipped a beat. There was no change of pecking order; we never had to work anything out. For years what was hers had been mine, and now, what was mine was automatically hers. I was delighted beyond measure to be able, at long last, to make a real contribution toward our well being.

In thirteen years, the number of serious arguments we have had could be counted on one hand, and every single one of those was prior to our stabilizing in Awakeness. We do not argue. We do not fuss. I don't know that I have ever raised my voice at her; I cannot recall her doing so to me. Maybe it has happened somewhere along the way, but if so it was a long time ago, I'm sure of that much.

I'm reporting this simply because I want to make it known that this kind of relationship is available. We both know it's reasonably rare, and we both know it doesn't have to be. When Betsy and I went to get our marriage license, the clerk of court asked, "So have either one of you been married before?"

Betsy and I shot each other a grin and then I said, "Let me put it this way. I'm her first husband, and she's my last wife." And so it is.

WAKING UP ROSEBUD

This short article is about a transformation that took place just recently. I'll call my friend Rosebud because she is finally flowering so beautifully after spending so much time in preparation. Mind you, Rose still has her work cut out for her. She's come to the end of seeking, but her awakening is merely an invitation to join all the rest of us Endless Dancers.

But I'm getting ahead of myself. A couple of weeks ago I got an email from a woman in Italy. Here's what she said:

> *Dear Fred-*
>
> *I'm a long timer-Much too long (35 yrs). So much clarity, so much understanding, that somehow doesn't click. Or it seems to many times but yet it does not.*
> *You well know this!!!*
> *Sometimes I feel I'm at my wit's end; I started out with Osho, and then and then and then.....*
> *I just read 2 of your books and listened to you on utube. What I feel is that you're able to bring light and (???) to what IS and not to what I'd want it TO BE.*
> *It is very moving, very humbling, very ordinary-sort of a soft ruthlessness.*
> *It's allowed me to own what I didn't want to and also let go of it.*
> *So YES if you're available I'd love to have a session with you.*
> *I live in Italy -so your morning is my afternoon.... (6 hrs difference)*
> *Please let me know and happy New Year (quite an auspicious moment to start off...) Love and Thank you,*
>
> *Rosebud*

The best line in her letter was the one where she said "soft ruthlessness." I showed that to Betsy and we both hooted over it because it was so perfectly on target. I tell the ruthless truth. When you call me, you get what you get. You may like it or you may not like it, but what you get is the truth.

Rosebud and I started our session and it went really well. Her sense of humor was a real plus and don't think this woman was anybody's little-old-lady. She was sharp as a tack! She saw everything very quickly and thoroughly. I thought she was a shoo-in. I had no idea that there would come a time in the next few minutes when I'd have to question whether she was going to wake up or not.

When we got to the end of Round One, I asked her a magical question, and she cracked as wide as sunrise. She couldn't speak. She laughed, she teared up, but she sputtered out that she couldn't say anything. She had seen, very, very clearly, what she was not. I asked her if she was confused, because confusion can be heavy in an Awakening Session, especially at that place. She shook her head no and whispered "Beyond confused."

"Blown?" I asked.

"Yes. Blown," she answered.

At this point the heavy lifting was—I assumed—essentially over. People who are really clear at the end of Round 1 will typically go on to to wake up more fully. So we took a short break, and when I returned to the computer I was in high spirits and chock full of confidence.

My session with Rosebud had come to the point at which I tell a potentially transformative story that I call "The Homecoming Story." For you old-timers out there, I once called it "The Void Story." It is as strong as death and has woken up more people than everything else I do combined.

For Rosebud, however, it was different. Two-thirds of the way through she stopped the story and with a shake of her head said, "I hear this. I know where you're going. I understand it intellectually, but I'm just not getting it."

There was a time when this would have driven me nuts. At that time, "The Homecoming" was not only the best arrow in my quiver, it was essentially the only arrow in my quiver because I had come to lean on it so heavily. Not anymore.

"Well, dear, this is where the ruthlessness comes in, because you don't just get to tell me that and then go away disappointed. It's too late. You've seen too much to go backwards now. We're going to investigate and we're going to find out if you're willing to tell yourself the truth or not. You told me you were ready to accept truth over comfort. Here's where we find out if you meant that when you said it."

I then began asking her a series of questions. "You've seen clearly that there is no Rosebud, isn't that right?"

"Yes."

"We looked for a Rosebud but couldn't find one anywhere, is that right?"

"Yes."

"Then tell me who is it that "understands this intellectually, but isn't getting it?"

She looked at me with a blank face.

"Isn't that Rosebud?" I asked her.

"Yes," she confessed. "It's Rosebud."

"Only there is no Rosebud, so it can't be Rosebud, isn't that right?"

"Yes."

"And there's no one else here, so who is it?"

"I don't know," she said.

"It's nobody," I told her. "That thought is arising, but no one is thinking it! Do you see this?"

"Oh!" she said as a light went on. "The one who doesn't exist is somehow in the way!"

"That's right!" I shouted. "There's no one having that thought, it's just arising on its own. It's just conditioning, like when a doctor hits your knee with a rubber hammer. Your leg's going to flip up. It's automatic. There's no thought to it. It's reflex. And every time the Rosebud who doesn't exist feels threatened, up comes this protective thought pattern. We could sit here all day, and it will just do it, and do it, and do it. You can't stop it and you can't make it go away, but do you have to believe it?"

"No," she told me.

I then took her through some additional inquiry, and within five minutes she'd woken up. She saw the truth very quickly and easily, and this time she accepted it. We went over some ramifications of her new "state," and I gave her a little general orientation to help her clear.

This morning I woke to find this letter in my inbox. What better way could you start your day?

Dear Fred

After the session I was (????? who knows), but I had to go to the kitchen and whilst before it would have been my aim and goal.... the kitchen.

Now there was this unbelievable understanding, and honouring of the "space" that linked the veranda to the kitchen...

And the walking in this space to "reach the kitchen".... And thus "treading space" so to speak.

This space – seeing it, noticing it, honouring it-is a miracle. Somehow, even though you point to it in your book, suddenly IT IS.

Well I could write a lot about it, but right now I'm just starting to get the feel of it.

Osho used to say don't listen to the words...listen to the gap. Or...

Heaven is on the way to heaven. - Yes indeed, lots of stuff learned and apparently understood is taking on new depth and meaning.

Dear Fred I could just cry and cry in this seeing. I heard you say or else you wrote that "you simply cannot imagine what's there for you". I believed you and stopped imagining, sort of giving up on expectations-just asking for the truth.

I don't know where I am now-still sort of dazed.

I do know however that something is unfolding and I'm not in a hurry because who would want to exchange this magic of spaciousness for a "finished product"-which is what we all seem to strive for but with no prize at the end!

So thank you and again thank you-for your clarity and depth,

your simple and funny "matter of factedness.." and for this.

Hope to hear you soon and I'll let you know of the next developments.

Love

Rosebud

KNOW IN THIS MOMENT

I received this comment recently from someone who follows my website, *Awakening Clarity Now.*

> *You have said, "As seekers, we want to experience Oneness objectively." Since the mind is an object and the concept of knowing is also an object, the idea that we can "know in this moment" that we are awake might warrant some more pointing.*

The writer is correct in suggesting that the *concept* of knowing something may be an object; however, no concept can arise prior to I Am. This I Am is neither a concept nor an object, and that which knows it is not mind. Mind itself is a concept appearing within I Amness.

When consciousness comes to consciously know itself—through the light of I Am and the sense of being—we call that movement "awakening." It is this to which we are referring when we speak in the conventional sense of "enlightenment." This "conventional enlightenment" is where nearly all nondual teachings point and includes most of what is said in this one. It's enough, it's plenty, and finding both clarity and stability within nondual awakening is what leads to "embodiment," which is generally considered to be the "end game" or the "point" of authentic nondual awakening.

However, except in imagination, neither awakening nor embodiment has anything to do with a so-called individual. It does not occur to or for an imaginary character. All presently awakened beings know this. If we have had an awakening experience and experienced brightness, but we have since had that brightness subside and are back to being cloudy, then we will have likely forgotten this fact.

Let us understand that the term embodiment does not mean that a so-called individual has now, at last, been cleared up. There's no one there to clear up; rather, embodiment means that our erroneous belief in a so-called individual has been cleared out or that this belief is at least well along in the apparent thinning process. In Clarity, nobody knows anything in any moment. Consciousness knows itself not through the mind but by being itself. That's Oneness.

We can safely say that I Am is everything, including both *you the imaginary character*, and *You the apparently real Conscious Awakeness*. I Am can also be called Oneness or, for the fussy, Not-twoness. I have taught this for years, and I don't now need to take any of that back. It is so.

And...

Those of us who move from unit to witness to Oneness may have a sense that Oneness is the end of the line. It certainly feels like that. It felt like that here for years. And for the great majority of us, that's going to be the truth—which is just fine. Nothing is being missed. Nothing is lacking. Nonetheless, while Oneness may be the end of "our" line, let us not become convinced that it is the end of "the" line. It is unless it isn't.

For some, for what has historically been a very small number within an already infinitesimal percentage of units, Oneness will simply be the end until it isn't. I suspect the number of those for whom it isn't the end of the line will start to climb significantly in the next few years, but I can't know this.

THE LAST VEIL

I love it when Life pulls things together, don't you? I had this happen recently in a delightful way. The subject around which things coalesced was the witness. I had been thinking over an article on the subject for quite some time, but before that happened, I had a Clarity Session with an interesting guy from Asheville, NC, who I'll call K. I had helped K wake up a few weeks before, and he woke up very very clearly. He'd done a lot of clearing prior to awakening; thus, he's making quite good progress within post-awakening—all in a very short while.

What I'm saying is that when K saw it, he really saw it. He was brightly awake when I left him at the end of our Awakening Session, and he was just about as brightly awake when we started our recent Clarity Session, and by the end, he was glowing like a light bulb. As Life would have it, what did K want to talk about in his Clarity Session? The witness! That's synchronicity.

Another example of synchronicity occurred last night, as I was writing this article, when I got an email from a client asking about the exact thing I had cut a video on just the evening before. I simply sent her a link to my video *On Presence...and Absence.* Score another one for God.

CAUTION, SELF-PROMOTION AHEAD:
This is why it's a good idea to subscribe to my YouTube channel. I currently have over 60 videos available, and one or another of them will answer almost every question I get, and I get a lot of questions, the great majority of which I simply don't have the time to answer, certainly not in detail. I can't begin to enumerate the number of times people have written to say, "I was just pondering so and so, and then your new video arrived out of the blue and cleared the whole thing up for me."

At any rate, these synchronicities show up in our lives all the time. It's a tease from formless Reality to Itself as form, meaning these human units it's wearing. Manifestation, however illusory we might hear that it is, can certainly be a laugh riot. Who would ever want want to transcend such a terrific opportunity for joy and love and simple surprise?

Well, yeah, I did for quite a while! Fine. I did what I did until I didn't. Now I know better, but back to synchronicity.

Synchronicity is the experience of two or more events being seen as meaningfully related, where they are unlikely to be causally related; nonetheless, the subject sees the coincidence as significant.

The concept of synchronicity was first described in the 1920s by Carl Jung, a Swiss psychologist. Jung is also the author of the amazing *Red Book*, a well-thumbed copy of which sits on my coffee table. Unbelievable art. More on Jung another time. Right now, it is enough to say that I am hit by synchronicity on a regular basis, and this witnessing coincidence with K is just the latest example.

The witness is not something we usually discuss in early awakening, simply because the depth of seeing that sparks interest in it often is not there. Granted, I certainly write and talk about the oneness of all, and I both illuminate and demonstrate this in session, but the more subtle aspects of oneness often go unseen for a while, sometimes for a very long while. My friend K, however, had the ears to hear; thus, he heard, and when something about his experience wasn't quite lining up, he wanted a closer look immediately, so he called me. You just have to admire that.

What I'm sharing with you is essentially what K and I talked about in his Clarity Session, not everything because we did a little Attention Practice and covered some other topics, but I'll give you the general takeaway from the bulk of our hour.

First off, if you don't know a lot about the witness state, then do a search on YouTube for my video on the subject, which is the best and fastest way I know of to enter it immediately, even if I did cut the video myself about the time *The Book of Undoing* came out. You can bet I would not have cut a half-hour video on something that was without value. The witness state is a big jump up from everyday awareness, so it can be incredibly useful in helping us to explore an alternative view of Reality.

I remember my stay there quite well and quite fondly. It lasted a good while. I also well remember the summer night years ago when my friend Scott Kiloby told me the truth about it. You could have knocked me over with a feather. Get ready, because that's what I'm going to do for you here.

We begin to experience the witness state when our identification with "little me" has begun to unravel and deteriorate. This is where the sense of detachment in the witness state initially comes from. Suddenly we're not taking things so seriously any more. Identifying with the Vastness instead of just the body and mind can be very freeing. We have moved from one side of the yin-yang circle to the other.

Before my awakening, I had been hoping that if and when realization came about, it would somehow help me to transcend my relative life, which was then sucking-out-loud. It didn't. What it did do, however, after a fine beginner's romp as Pure Nondual Awareness, was give me some distance from it, which probably saved my life. Awakening didn't solve my problematic life situation and it didn't catapult me out of it, but it did allow me to see that the lousy life content I was suffering from didn't belong to me. It was Fred's mess, and screw him! I was just the witness.

This is an example of the detachment that can be experienced from the witness state. This is also the level of realization that's been seen by a lot of folks who are in the "no one here and nothing to do" stage. It can be a confusing time—it was for me—but with luck it's just a stage we'll eventually pass through. However much "nondual experiencing" is showing up for us, it always feels like the whole thing. That's one of the hallmarks of an authentic awakening, but it's probably one of the hallmarks of an inauthentic awakening experience as well, so I wouldn't go to the bank on this feeling.

Until we have begun to see deeply enough to recognize that we don't know a damn thing, fresh openings usually run sort of like this: "OH!!! YES!! NOW I see! THIS is the truth! Of COURSE! I used to think I knew the truth, but I see now that I only knew some of the truth, even though I thought I saw all of the truth. It's a good thing I SEE IT ALL now."

Or other innocent bullshit to that same effect.

We always know what we know, but we never know what we don't know. If we can keep this little maxim in mind, we may be able to stay open and humble enough to receive more, and more, and more. I think the reason I am able to maintain some modicum of humility—in this one area—is because it plays to my sense of greed: be small, grow larger. It's a bit of a paradox.

There's no end to opening if we don't end it ourselves. I ran across something by Meister Eckhart, the 13th and 14th Century

Christian mystic, that spoke of "the humility of our perplexity" and this is what he was talking about—knowing that we don't know. But what a turn of phrase!

What is the witness, anyway? What can we know about it?

What we call the witness or the witness state is simply the first-hand experience that "I am not my character." We see/feel/intuit what we are not. It's like you've been pulling a cart your whole life, and suddenly it's released. It generally feels quite "mystical," or at least it did for me. We move from unsuccessful seeker to partially successful finder. As mentioned above, the good news about this breakthrough is the same as the bad news: it feels like that's all there is to get. It's not.

Seeing through everyday life, what we can call relativity, is not a life strategy. We can't live a negative; we can't live what we're not. We can, however, know that something big has happened, that we're absolutely on the right track, and that if we behave, then more will surely follow. That is an example of a successful takeaway from the witness state.

The witness state is almost surely going to first show up as an intermittent experiencing. As a rule, this will then be followed by its gradually showing up more and more and/or for longer and longer. I remember when I could willfully move from the witness to Fred, back and forth, like it was a toggle switch. That was very comforting and encouraging.

And then things began to get a little dry. This is the problem with trying to live a negative—trying to live what we are not, instead of trying to live as we are. We may become subject to listlessness, depression and nihilism—WTF? Who cares? It's no fun.

So, to help you stay out of that mire, let me share with you the secret identity of the witness, the bit of Truth I learned from Scott Kiloby years ago. We were talking, and I brought up the witness. He let me finish my observations and then said quietly, "Fred, the witness is a thought." The instant I heard that it shot through my brain and body like a blazing sky rocket. I remember nearly falling down.

I was so ripe! That's what Scott knew better than I did. Teachers can often sense when we're on the edge of something, and then they can nudge us toward the gate. I flew through it! This was the second piece of the puzzle. This was what had been missing. When I initially woke up, I moved from the dark side of the yin-yang to the light side. I didn't actually give up my identity, I just moved it from identification with the relative to identification with the Absolute. I went from being Fred to being not-Fred.

I, however, am Oneness. I am the whole thing. I am both sides. I am the full circle. And so are you.

My friend K had an inkling of this truth. Like many others have done, he told me that he'd been experiencing the witness state since his awakening, but he was now beginning to sense that it was some sort of a provisional truth, not a complete truth. And of course he was right.

When K asked me to help him out with the now-suspect witness, I did not launch into a lecture. I said, "Let me show you." We then commenced an hour of Attention Practice that went further and deeper than I imagined it would. Fine. What happens happens. Check out my Attention Practice video. It's a good way into the witness, and it's also a good way out of it.

And watch out for those synchronicities. They are one of life's great giggles.

GRATITUDE

DIVINE EXPRESSION AND THE FOUNDATION OF CLARITY

OR

HAPPY NONDUAL THANKSGIVING

If I had to test someone's level of awakeness, and I could look at but one thing, it would surely be the measure of their gratitude. That is the foundation, indeed the very cornerstone upon which clarity rests.

I'm not talking about someone's declared thankfulness for their relative conditions, the sort that people across the United States express on Thanksgiving day. This type of relative thankfulness can be important on a unit level and beyond, and it's something that can and should be willfully nurtured, but such gratitude is still about an apparent individual's satisfaction and surrender within the Dreaming. The type of gratitude I'm talking about here is deep, very deep—as deep as it gets. I am talking about absolute gratitude, causeless gratitude, an all-encompassing, all-embracing, wondrous joy at the key feature, the very definition of consciousness: the knowledge that "I Am."

The first two verses of the Tao Te Ching tell us, "The Tao that can be named is not the eternal Tao." Lao Tzu could have stopped right there; he'd already given us the key to seeing/being reality as it is. But he, in his time, like me in mine, found it totally irresistible to at least try to step beyond language—while using languaging as his tool to do so. It's nuts, but Lao Tzu was not calling "his" shots, and neither am I calling "mine."

Among all the words Lao Tzu expended in pointing to the

unnameable are subtle suggestions about something else, a more fundamental truth than even the Unnamed. However, though he had surely tasted this truth, rather than drive us crazy for the next 2,500 years by trying to tell us about that which cannot be told, he wisely only hinted that prior to the challenging Mystery of the Unnamed there is the essentially impenetrable Mystery of the Great Unborn.

Lao Tzu was smart enough to leave that puppy alone. I am not.

That which exists prior to and after the arising and falling of consciousness does not know itself. It has no desire to know itself, for it has no desire, not even the desire to be. It is an indescribable, yet intuitable and, for lack of a better word, tasteable state which, for us, is beyond comprehension or communication. This is why I knew this article was doomed to failure before I even sat down. Still, it's so much fun to try, and in trying to do the impossible I will be making some statements that appear to contradict what some other teachers are saying, but let's be broad enough to at least accept the possibility that what other teachers say and what I say could both be true. Perhaps we are just talking about different segments of the same orange. I find that the inclusive "both/and" versus "either/or" is most often the way of it for what we discover in the deeper end of the spirituality pool.

All nondual teachings rightly emphasize consciousness. They may call it presence or awareness, aware space, or something else, but they generally agree that consciousness is the non-thing that all objects appear to, and the thrust of the teachings is to get seekers to shift their focus off the content of the manifestation and onto the unmanifested consciousness that recognizes the manifestation. That is the great first stage in spiritual growth. I am no mathematician, but it seems to me that our concept of the absence of manifestation, what nondualists refer to as the "unmanifested," has much the same relationship to manifestation that zero has to numbers. It is less a "something" unto itself than it is an indication of a "nothing" in relation to things which are more real than itself. The next great step in spiritual growth is to recognize that the manifested is made of the unmanifested. There are not two things. Yes, as many teachers assert, the show of manifestation, together with a concept of the absence of manifestation, is made of consciousness; however, not all is conscious.

Prior to consciousness there is what we will wrongly, but aptly, term Noneness. We might first imagine that Noneness is the opposite of Oneness, but even though that notion seems to make sense, it is untrue. Neither Noneness nor Oneness has an opposite. Noneness has no opposite because it is beyond existing or not existing, beyond being or not-being. Oneness has no opposite because it is all that actually IS, and Oneness or Sense of Being, as anyone who has done an Awakening Session with me knows first-hand, is the mother of all experience.

And no, I am neither confused, nor am I alluding to any sort of duality. Oneness is all there IS, but prior to Oneness there lies the empty, alive potentiality for all that IS—Noneness. That Noneness is the Source of consciousness, and consciousness is the source of What Is. Noneness can be imagined as a light that constantly shines but is itself invisible. What it does is light up whatever it hits. In and of itself, it is nothing, but without it, nothing else can be. Consider this light to be our Source but not because it creates anything. It is pure potential: nonmaterial, nonpersonal, and nonexistent. It is not a zero because it does not function in relation to anything else. It is not an absence because to be absent you have to be something in the first place. Noneness is sheer possibility and as such it is the source of all. The light of possibility must shine at all times for anything to Be or Become, including consciousness. When ever-shining Source meets ever-amenable mind, consciousness is born.

And here enters spontaneous gratitude, because this is the great wonder of wonders, the sudden mind-expanding, mind-blowing Knowing that all else pales beside. It is positively explosive—you might do worse than to imagine the Big Bang. From nothing springs everything, in a blinding flash so short and sudden as to be nearly incalculable. From potentiality to apparent actuality—bam!—I Am!

Wow.

This I Am-ness, this I Am-ing, is the first dream, the first wave of the Dreaming—the first hallucination after the ether takes hold. But I Am is a magnificent Dreaming. The detail is astounding. The vastness is unimaginable. The excitement and boredom, joys and sorrows, successes and failures, awe and horror, fear and desire—oh! What a time is had by All.

Human beings are almost always more interested in the content of the dream than they are the identity of the dreamer. We want to know all about what's happening in our dream, while overlooking who it's happening to. Our questions and doubts are endless, because in their absence we'd have to tell ourselves the obvious truth.

I Am! What a miracle!

I Am! This is perfect!

I Am! It leaves me dumbstruck!

That dumbstruck awe at simply being is the wellspring of fundamental gratitude. The gratitude for knowing I Am, when it would be so easy for us not to be at all. It's crazy, it's splendid, it's What Is on a plane where there is no "what isn't." Cool!

And prior to I Am?

Ah, you got that, did you not? Very good.

Prior to I Am, I Am That which I can only point to with a blundering finger—and so are you. Only we don't know we are until we do.

To those of you who are Americans near or far, Happy Thanksgiving! To everyone else, take a thanks-giving day anyway!

Thanksgiving
2014

BEFORE THE BEGINNING

IT TELLS ITS STORY

Before the beginning, It Is.

After the ending, It Is.

Between the beginning and the ending, between the ending and the beginning, always, It Is, offering infinite potentiality.

Prior to the arising of I Amness, It does not know Itself. It is beyond existing or not existing. There is neither a presence nor an absence of I Amness.

Presence or absence do not apply. No opposites apply.

Birth and death are opposites but there is no opposite to Life.

Before the beginning, before any appearance arises, It Is. After all appearances go, It Is.

It neither comes nor goes. It is the Source of all that comes and goes. It is the Source of Beingness.

Prior to the arising of Beingness, It does not feel Itself. There is neither a presence nor an absence of Beingness. Even so, It Is. It neither rises nor falls, never lives or dies. It is Beyond. Presence or absence do not apply. Even so, It Is.

It never is not. It Is That Which Has No Name.

In the beginning, at the birth of a human, there immediately arises Universal Amness. Joy, gratitude, elation, awe, and wonder abound.

Universal Amness is without center or boundary, name or form, size or weight, duration or volume, preference or personality. It is the ever-flowing, boiling, booming verbness of Life.

It is always in movement, metamorphosing, growing without expanding, shrinking without diminishing, as perfectly harmonized as an atomic clock, while appearing chaotic and unstable.

Freshly born from the Unborn, space and time appear on it, within it: upon their mating, infinite combinations of yin and yang are birthed. Endless zeroes, endless ones. Endless blacks and whites, sunrises and sunsets, males and females, and on and on and on.

Dreaming without a dreamer.

Soon, within Universal Amness, the I-sense arises, initially so furtive and hidden that it is like a cloud within a mist. Yet slowly, steadily, spontaneously, inexorably it knits itself from sensations, perceptions.

Universal Beingness is coming to sense Itself, but as yet this sensing is pure. The Tree of Knowledge has not yet been discovered and its dangerous fruit not yet eaten.

Perfection reigns briefly, while thought lies ready in the shadows.

Two years beyond birth—within the light of the false dawn of apparent individual self-awareness— comes the energetic blast of an enormous, instantaneous contraction. Much like the Big Bang, only rushing inward instead of outward, all things and all attention are sucked into a center, surrounding a miniscule pinhead of a human unit, until finally, with excited elation and utter confusion, Universal Beingness comes to believe "I Am this human being."

Personal I Amness has arisen.

Indra's Net, that infinite, alive, divine mesh thrown across the universe by the King of the Hindu Gods, forgets its true nature, forgets its own divinity, and comes to believe it is a single jewel in a single intersection, and not the net itself.

But notions of either/or do not apply. I Amness is both the jewel and the net. The tendency is to remember the one while excluding the other. We transfer identification from one ghost to the other.

Oscillation. Misidentification.

In the beginning, I Am the primary arising. I come first. Then, as I come to know Myself through the hands and eyes of conditioned space, I get lost in the appearance of multiplicity within my Unity. I forget that I Am the singular arising. I Am.

Whether I remember myself or not, I Am.

Although personal I Amness appears to arise, it does not. It is just a thought. When this thought is seen through, we call it awakening, but there is no awakening for the personal I Amness because it never arose to begin with. A thought bubble pops.

When the personal I Amness appears to fall, as all arisings do, there is no death. That which does not live to begin with cannot die.

A light flickers out.

Whence the light?

Wax does not know itself but that does not mean that it is dead or that it is not there. It forms many shapes and sizes of candle. It is the Source of all candles, and thus it is the Source of all light.

Each being is a wick for Universal Amness. Each human being is a wick for Personal I Amness. When Life, the divine energy, meets a human unit, the offspring of that meeting is consciousness.

So long as that wick burns, It knows Itself truly, while pretending to not know itself. Even so, It Is.

When a wick has burned itself out, the light from that candle goes out. Nothing less, nothing more. The inexhaustible wax is unaffected. It Is, but It does not know Itself.

What to say about wax? Nothing. What to think about wax? Nothing. It is prior to consciousness and consciousness cannot touch it, cannot know it.

We can know of It. We can be It. We can't not be it. Universal I Amness is an arising, a shadow of the Real.

What to say about wicks? Not much. They are empty arisings. They are neither conscious nor unconscious. They are mechanisms for transporting fuel. They are the tools that transform Potential into Beingness—so long as they burn.

What to say about flame? The nature of flame is to cast light, to cast the light of Beingness from the Source of all Beingness, which is prior to, and beyond, this world.

Flame!

I Am!

I Am the primary arising. I do not need this world, for I Am with or without this world. I know Myself and then I don't, but I never diminish or disappear.

I Am Everything.

I Am Nothing.

Source is beyond either.

I do not need this world, but this world desperately needs Me.

Without the sense of Being, nothing can exist, for it can't be known without Me. I Am First.

I Am the only Power in the universe. I Am Omnipotence.

I do not need this world, but nothing can exist here unless I presently know it. The entire universe is contingent upon my Being. I have to know, and do know, everything everywhere at all times. Objects, beings and arisings endure only for so long as I know them. At my briefest inattention they immediately wither.

I Am the only Knowing in the universe. I Am Omniscience.

I do not need this world, but I am its Keeper. I have to know everything everywhere at all times, or it cannot be. In order to know everything everywhere at all times, I have to Be everywhere at all times.

I Am the only Being. I Am Omnipresent.

And finally,

of course,

I am you.

You Are It.

ALPHA-OMEGA

This symbol, which is effectively the new "logo" for The Living Method of Awakening, is composed of the Classical Greek letters for Alpha and Omega—the first and last letters of the Greek alphabet in upper case—and a laurel wreath. These letters have historically been used to represent "beginning and ending," or in more casual usage in Western traditions and literature "from A to Z." In some translations of the New Testament, Jesus is said to refer to himself as "the Alpha and Omega." If he said it, then he surely meant the same thing I'm indicating, but I certainly don't use it here as a Christian reference.

This teaching uses the symbol to refer to your True Nature; however, I may be using the term True Nature in a way that you do not. Of course, in general forums and in general speech, when I say "True Nature," it is essentially a synonym for Oneness, which is the same way that most people use it. And it's true—you are indeed Oneness—All-That-Is-As-It-Is. That's as far as I normally go because it's as far as I need to go and it's the end of the line in terms of Self-knowledge that will add anything to your life as a unit through which Conscious Awakening is functioning.

We have all heard that there's "nothing in awakening for the ego," and that's certainly true. But that's not the same thing as saying there's nothing in awakening for the apparent hosting unit. Not by a long shot! Awakeness, which experiences Itself through the Fred unit is having a blast. And much of the time that feels like joy within and for this unit. I know it's all stories, but don't let anyone tell you that a bad story is as much fun as a good one. They are equal and empty, but they are not the same.

However, in some discussions, chiefly in Clarity Sessions and very rarely in articles like this, when I use the words "True Nature" I am speaking of That from which Oneness sprang. I will, in surrender to the fact that there is no adequate term, from this point forward, refer to That as either "Noneness," or "That" interchangeably. This topic is not a common one and will probably not become a common one for me either, but who knows? So sit up straight and listen close—I will not be answering emails asking for further clarification.

When writing for a wide audience, I usually stay away from this subject because it can be confusing to the reader. I don't want to turn a bunch of awakening beings back into seekers who think they've missed something. Regardless of where you are, you haven't missed a thing.

My comments on this subject can also appear to contradict my own Oneness teachings as well as those of other teachers, but in fact they do not. As ever in nondual spirituality, when the mind is seeking for the either/or answer to something, it's inevitably discovered that the proper answer is both/and. You can already see how confusing this topic can be and can sense why I and the not-numerous others who know of it steer away from the subject. But I notice it's at the top of the topic pile today.

Even while writing this article, I'm reserving the same right that I reserve for every other act that is taken through the Fred unit: the right to change or condemn any and all of it as early as the minute I finish it. I am writing from this present clarity; it's the best anyone can ever do. It should not, however, be confused with Truth; it's simply as close as I can get—thus far. Here we go.

Prior to active Consciousness, there exists what we will call latent Consciousness. When latent Consciousness is the only state presenting, It does not know Itself. Nevertheless, It Is. Another way to say this is that prior to Oneness, Noneness Is. It is the Still, Silent Witness of manifestation, which is not other than It, but which in no way equals It.

Since one of my favorite hobbies is using double negatives when writing or talking about nondual philosophy, I will say that Noneness cannot not exist, yet there is no opposite for it, the way there is at least a mental opposite for terms like "manifest" (unmanifest) or "form" (emptiness). We are talking about a state beyond either of those.

When a sentient being spontaneously appears to arise from Noneness, a chemical reaction takes place. No one does it, it just happens. When latent Consciousness comes into contact with a reasonably developed brain, the chemical child of the pairing is active Consciousness. I-Amness begins, although it is Universal I-Amness, and thus without specific identity. We might call this simply "Amnessing."

In a human being, however, the chemical reaction continues to roll out in a very special way. Beginning at about the age of two, when self-awareness begins to dawn on a child, Oneness starts to identify as that single unit! Oneness has made a Faustian trade, giving all of Wholeness for the sake of apparent individuality, and it thinks it's made a hell of a deal. Indeed. By the way, I am not limiting Conscious Awareness to human beings; I simply am not addressing any other beings.

In unusual cases—too frequent to be called rare and too infrequent to be labeled common—this individual identification starts to unwind. It's less likely to happen when a unit is experiencing one great arising after another—although it sometimes happens in the case of highly developed, insightful units at the top of their game who, even though they are enjoying the fruits of an extremely successful unit, manage to notice that they're still not satisfied and are not going to get there by adding another zero to their bank balance or another notch to their bedfellow stick.

There are always a few other types of exceptions, but as is the norm with me, I am chiefly interested in a Big Number teaching—what's happening with the most people most of the time.

In line with that goal, I note that the common denominator which drives us to the point where we are reduced to reading articles like this one, diving into books that the general population wouldn't touch with a ten-foot pole, or watching videos by nondual teachers until we're haunted by them in our sleep, is suffering. That's what brought the Fred unit into the fold, and the odds are good that it's what brought you here, too. You don't get a laurel wreath for wanting to avoid suffering.

Strangely, however, some say you get one if you make it through the often-accused-of-being-mythical Gateless Gate. Even more strangely, however, should this blessed event occur, we discover that there is no place to hang the wreath, no one who made it through the Gate, and thus no one to reward. I don't have a wreath, but the giant bronze bust of Socrates (who looks suspiciously like Plato to me) that I have in my living room has one. Good for him! The only catch is that he had to drink poison to get it, and he only received it a long time after he was dead. I'm out on that program.

So what happens to Conscious Awareness upon the death of an individual unit? One jewel in Indra's Net gets dark and quiet, as it drops back into a latent state. Trust me, there's nowhere for

Oneness to "go"—not even to Noneness. The channel on the Big Screen changes. Life goes on. And on and on and on...

All is well.

As for the laurel wreath, they have traditionally been given as symbols of triumph, victory, and achievement. In the ancient Western world they were given to emperors, great poets, Olympic champions, et al. It is used here more in line its other historical context, as the transition to eternal life—what might erroneously be called "victory" over death.

But we're not hanging it on any unit's head! Dead or alive, a unit is, on its own as empty as a crushed can—and just about that wise, too. That inherent emptiness, however, does not stop units from vying for gold stars, gold wreaths, or any other symbol of acclaim. Such things seem to mean a great deal to the one who isn't even there. Go figure.

Fredness, at first glance, appears to have come to nondual philosophy via the East—primarily teachings that began or moved through India, China, and Japan. I frankly thought they had a monopoly on it. They don't, even though some of the Greeks benefited from Indian and Egyptian teachings, and Western philosophy itself was preserved by early Islam during the Dark Ages.

The teachers who have given me the greatest help in coming to whatever level of clarity that's currently being experienced here are neither exclusively Eastern nor exclusively Western—they're both, which is perfect. Earliest on there was that confounding character of Jesus, whom I spent a lot of energy criticizing until I started spending it trying to figure out what he said and represented. Then came the ancient Zen masters, who shared a great deal before somehow birthing Eckhart Tolle into my life. He was the original game changer.

Then came Nisargadatta from the East and Adyashanti from the West. Ramakrishna, the Easterner, bowed out but not before he'd kindly introduced me to Byron Katie, the Westerner. Asian Ramana pointed to European Socrates and vice versa. Emerson's influence on me was birthed by Thoreau, whom I've neglected to place in between Jesus and the ancient Zen masters. Pardon me, Henry.

So I am staking a claim here for a non-geographically oriented teaching. When I say "unaligned," I mean it all across the board. What's happening here is not the standard nondual fare that the spiritual marketplace is already choked with; on the contrary, it remains so alien that the greater Western populace, the silent majority who are not in the "nondual choir" cannot even approach it, much less fathom it. Nor does it bear much kinship with what's going on in most areas of the celebrated wisdom traditions.

This post, clearly, is being written for the choir, "my choir" so to speak, to explain what's going on here—as if I knew!

Good Lord. I was going to do a short little explanatory article, and I notice this one is over 1,800 words. Can you say, "Out of control?" Clearly the typing should stop already.

So, in summation, what the new Living Method logo symbolizes (I think that's how this article started) is That which Is before the beginning and Is beyond the end, and Is beyond either. Alpha-Omega. Think of it simply as Home.

I'M AWAKE! WHAT DO I DO NOW?

Once we've had a nondual breakthrough we discover we are on new ground. Whether our penetration was a momentary glimpse, a flashy angels-and-trumpets event, or something in between those two, our most pressing question is typically "What do I do now?".

In an effort to be my sister and brother's keeper, let me tell you that this question is most often asked by ego in the immediate aftermath of awakening. It's *just* been seen that "our ego" is simply part of the dream and that it cannot, on the highest level, even be said to exist. In my case it was seen very clearly that there was no Fred Davis. So, even though we have *just* experienced the universal living truth of Oneness, which immediately smashes all notions of separation, nonetheless amid all of that stir, guess who shows back up?

Ego. Our character. It—our character—may not really exist; regardless, it *functions* as if it does. And we still have to deal with it. No matter how awake we get, our experience is that we are hung with the unit. I can sense that heads are already starting to ache, so let me jump in and explain myself the best I can.

When awakening occurs, what wakes up—as most of you know—is Awakeness itself—and *only* Awakeness itself. Given that there *is no* genuine free-standing ego that exists, it can't possibly be woken up. If there is no sleeping Fred, there cannot be an awake Fred.

The unmanaged body and thought patterns will continue to run until they don't. They have never been under your control, and they're certainly not going to be now that you're awake. You will, however, have a much better eye for your own unskillful patterns and thus it may look like things get worse before they get better.

I am talking about *years* of clearing, not weeks or months. Most patterns have to be seen through individually. Until they are, there will be egoic functioning. There's no one home, but it sure *looks like* there is to an outsider, and sometimes even to you, the "insider."

Having said all of this, which most of you have heard me say a lot of times before, let me now say that character-clouded Awakeness, though the means of a unit, can and does ask its more clear reflection, through the character of a teacher "What do I do now?"

It's a bit of a paradox, is it not? It is. And it is that critical paradox that we will address in this post. What is meant is, "How do I—the Awakeness that is now awake to my True Nature—stay clear?"

What are the skillful means at our disposal that can facilitate clearing out the mountainous remnants of our dream character that remain in post-awakening? I fully realize that there's no one there to have anything at its hypothetical disposal. No matter. So long as it *feels* like there's someone there, I'm suggesting that you *act as if* someone's there. You're going to do it unconsciously anyway, so why not do it consciously?

This immediately gets you out of that head and into that life. Clearing is not an activity of the brain. We can't think our way clear. Thus moving from the realm of thought to the realm of action is, in effect, the beginning of waking *down*, down out of the mind-story of division and into the apparent manifestation that is generally referred to as reality. That apparent reality is actually occurring *within* Reality, but one step at a time.

Here's a review of *The Book of Undoing* that was posted on Amazon yesterday, and which I just noticed while I was writing this post. Funny how that works...

> good but don't forget to....
> *ByGambit on May 26, 2015*
> *Format: Kindle EditionVerified Purchase*
> *You can have an awaking or a glimpse of it; it's very easy if you follow Fred's directions.*
>
> *However.....awakening will not last very long if the emotional body (another term is the pain body) hasn't been cleaned & transformed.*
>
> *That's why I also use releasing (as taught by Lester Levenson) and other resources such as Tom Stone's Technic.*
>
> *The ego is trying to run away to the "non-dual" state and doesn't want to deal with the emotional body (pain body). So read this book, enjoy it, enjoy the*

> *awakening state but keep working also on clearing your*
> *emotional body....*
> *I'll note that the author does advise his clients to*
> *work on "embodiment" by clearing the out the blockages*
> *from the emotional body.*

The reviewer makes a good point, one which I harp on all the time. Waking up is really wonderful and powerful, but it's only an *invitation* to the *real* dance of abidance and embodiment. It's the most important shift we ever make, but if it's the *last* shift we make, then a golden opportunity has been wasted and sleepy-time is dead ahead.

At the end of Awakening Sessions I will usually answer the "What do I do now?" question *twice*. First I answer in the same way I began this article—by pointing out to Awakeness that ego has just come in the back door and is now asking about how to best direct its free agency, about how to manage something that *isn't*—an independent life-on-its-own. I can't say this happens *every* time, but it does happen a great deal of the time.

Should that occur, I'll then lead them through some additional clearing material until the preposterous idea of dream management is seen through clearly again, and then finally come back to answer "What' do I do now?" in a practical manner. I offer them three tools to work with, which I now offer to you: my videos, self-inquiry on a moment-to-moment basis, and a specific meditation which I discuss and demonstrate in these two YouTube videos.

The Sense of Being Meditation
30 Minute Guided Meditation: Falling Into the Sense of Being

If you read the works of Nisargadatta Maharaj beyond the ubiquitous *I Am That,* you will hear him say over and over again, "Simply dwell on the I Am" or "Meditate on the I Am—it will open the door to everything else." He never gives instructions as to what that means, but if he had, they would sound much like the instructions I offer for The Sense of Being Meditation. To make it short and simple: you are practicing being Yourself. You are not sitting in order to be clear in some story of future but in order to be clearer here and *now*.

I recommend my videos to clients because they are very clear and, given that I just woke that person up, I know they can "hear" me. I can't tell you how huge this is. Don't try to listen to someone you're not drawn to or someone you used to be drawn to but aren't now. Listen to whom you resonate with *today*. You'll know them when you find them. If my approach doesn't appeal to you, change the channel—no hard feelings. It's not so much about "who *has* it?" as it is "who can *hear* it?" Most of us have specialized ears.

Moment-to-moment inquiry means living in inquiry. When you hear yourself say, "That shouldn't be," ask yourself "Who said that?" Can you trace that thought backwards and actually find an *owner* to it? Answering that from your head will do you no good whatsoever. You have to take the action and hit the wall. You have to show yourself that there's "no Fred" over and over and over again.

You can also ask yourself "Is that true?" Is it true that something that *is* "shouldn't" be? No. Never.

Is it true that something that isn't "should" be? Nope. Never ever.

We don't have to understand Life, but we *do* have to surrender to it whether we do so willingly or go down swinging. What happens is what happens. Of course, you are always free to suffer first and *then* surrender to it; I'm just trying to give you some options.

THE CASE FOR RATIONAL AWAKENING

"It seems that, in order to enlighten an Occidental, dissertations are, within a certain measure that is strictly limited, necessary.

Doubtless the ultimate, the real point of view, cannot be expressed in words, and the master would injure the pupil if he allowed him to forget that the whole problem lies precisely in jumping the ditch which separates truth which can be expressed from real knowledge. But the Occidental needs a discursive explanation to lead him by the hand to the edge of the ditch."

Hugo Benoit
French Psychiatrist & Eastern Philosopher
1904-1992

The reason that I don't direct this teaching more toward "how to awaken" is that it's simply not an efficient way for us to spend our time together. There's nothing, absolutely nothing that we need to do, learn, or know in order for us to wake up. That's because we are already awake. This "we" I refer to as being already awake includes you, the present consciousness reading this post, the same consciousness which will almost surely and erroneously also be thinking that it is the unit it is wearing—some mythical individual you which doesn't really exist.

Strangely, everything we, as apparently individual units, need to undo and unknow in order to consciously recognize our True Nature can take place in about two hours. Yep. I know this to be a fact because I watch it happen several times a week, and have been doing so for the better part of three years. I call this process Rational Awakening. While awakening itself may not be what we call rational, the necessary deconditioning leading to it can be, The Living Method of Spiritual Awakening being the present prime example of how this can be accomplished.

Given that it's now possible to bring about initial awakening so swiftly, a higher, truer, simpler, more efficient and enjoyable way of seeing and being is suddenly available to large crowds of people. And it will will continue to be available. Even this unit is not so self-centered and stupid as to think itself the end of the line. More is coming or, more probably, is already here, if as yet unannounced.

If people really want to wake up, and have left some room for precious doubt in their current belief system, it's actually hard for them not to wake up. Not waking up is the new exception. Rational Awakening is both reliable and predictable, which flies full in the face of nearly everything we've heretofore known.

By the way, the final step in moving into the truth of unity from the dream of separation, what we might presently call "an irrational jump," is actually just the turnaround of finally telling ourselves the truth about the truth. It's more like addiction recovery than anything else I know. I had a woman wake up last week in the first three minutes of our session—a new record, ego tells me. Within a week I had another woman wake up in the first twenty minutes—after starting out cheerful, but genuinely resistant. In the process of turning around her attitude, I accidentally woke her up a bit early—except that there are no accidents.

Of course, when I say, "I need for someone to be willing to tell themselves the truth," I say it knowing full well that there's no one there to do that. It's not an actual doing. It's more of an attitude than anything else, and its presence depends solely upon whether Oneness is ready to see through your particular character yet or not. There's nothing personal in it.

If you're ready, good for you; that's just as things should be, but there's nothing for you to be proud about. If you're not ready, good for you; you want to sleep a little longer, but you're using me as a snooze alarm, as in, "Not right now, but soon!" This teaching, however, is not a perpetual snooze alarm. Hang around and it will get under your skin. That, too, is just as it should be.

I was sitting in my living room this morning reading and pondering, and it struck me how Plotinus, the Roman philosopher-mystic who lived nearly two millenniums ago, St.

John of the Cross, the 16th century Christian mystic, and Sri Ramana Maharshi, the 20th century Hindu saint all recommendded the use of negative inquiry in order to discover your True Nature. Lots of others did as well, but this just happened to be the three I was thinking about this morning.

It was great advice that they handed down to us, I heartily recommend it as well, and strangely, it's turned out to be a big part of this teaching. What I have to offer is stories and questions. If you want answers, turn only to yourself. There's nothing mystical about what I do. It's as rational as arithmetic, but it's counter-intuitive, which generally leads to some client confusion along the way. But since that confusion is the calling card of clarity, all comes up sunny in the end.

Let me tell you a secret. This is an open secret, no one's been hiding it from us, but very few humans have actually discovered it. Most who have made the discovery have simply stumbled upon it, but that doesn't have to be the case for you. The secret?

It's not hard to recognize your True Nature, and it doesn't require a lot of time. I've helped tons of long-term seekers, people who've flown all over the world for retreats and spent crazy money for decades in a failed attempt to wake up, sit there in front of me on Skype amazed and dumbstruck. I can't know what the future may bring, but I think at least one branch of it is going to be powerfully influenced by a new wave of different forms of Rational Awakening.

There are, however, two flies in this wonderful ointment. The first is that very few people will put aside what they think they know long enough to discover what they don't know. My working hypothesis is that this is not a mistake. I'm not saying it's a plan, but I'm saying it's not a mistake. The chief reason I hold this hypothesis is that I can't actually find any mistakes around here, and whenever I have a hypothesis that lines up with What Is, though I know that there can be contrary opinions, I also know that no actual evidence that can be presented against my claim.

What Is rules. It's a comfort.

However, the second fly in the ointment is that while recognizing our True Nature is relatively easy, it is rather difficult for us to accept what we see when we see the truth. It is nigh onto impossible to move from recognition into acceptance by our lonesomes. People do it, but not many, and my interest has always been in Big Numbers Spirituality: what works for the highest percentage of the people the highest percentage of the time.

Here's a big number for you: 100% of the people I talk with

privately who are willing to tell themselves the truth will wake up. Some aren't willing, but even figuring in the ones who aren't willing, it turns out that better than 90% of the people who talk to me do indeed wake up.

I don't talk about this number much because it's so ridiculous. If a Fred had anything to do with that sort of precision, it would doubtless go to his head as such things always do with boundless egos, thus rendering him entirely useless as a spiritual vehicle. Fortunately I've seen clearly that there is no Fred, so we needn't worry about him bragging his way into unconsciousness. Today's typist is an empty little pawn of Oneness.

Truly, in an attempt to be accurate, not modest, I can say that this is a quite ordinary, everyday, garden variety unit that contrary to common sense is presently inhabited and consciously utilized by the extraordinary truth of our Being. It has been "drawn"—meaning pushed, pulled, and prodded—to sit down and type this whether it wants to or not. It had other plans, but out the window they went.

These units do what they do until they do something else, for the simple reason that they cannot not do it. There is no such thing as "why." Pursuing the "why" will drive you crazy, but once again you are invited to find that out for yourself. I did.

We are not actually mystically separated from our True Nature. That is, in fact, a literal impossibility. People tell me they can't find their True Nature, and I have to tell them that I can't find anything else. If they are "drawn" to spend a bit of time talking to what's coming through this nifty body puppet, they will almost inevitably come to agree with me. They will have seen and accepted on quite a broad sliding scale, the overwhelming fact of their obviousness. Poof.

Clearing is always a challenge, no matter how we wake up. Many of us spend decades clearing prior to awakening, only to find out that we will have to clear up a second time in post-awakening, primarily to wipe the slate clean of what we thought was clearing us in pre-awakening. The whole business is frustrating on one hand but incredibly rewarding on the other. Of course it's not actually about progress. We all have to do what we have to do, but if we're open and alert, we may not have to keep on doing what we've had to do in the past.

Three years ago I had a Biblical-style vision where I saw an endless line of spiritual pilgrims being directed up my apartment's stairwell via conventional spiritual strategies. The idea was to reach "the landing," which was where enlightenment was hiding out. In a flash I saw that nearly all of the pilgrims were dying on the steps. Very few made it to the top. Everyone was dying "on the way to God."

A nearly blinding pair of questions arrived in this brain.

"What if we could wake them up first?"

"What if we could start them out on the landing and then lead them down the steps to clear?"

I could see that it could be a total revolution. It had the ability to turn everything on its head. And because it was fast, it would be able to reach vast numbers, regardless of their age or background. All that was required was an open mind and a willingness to tell ourselves the truth. Familiarity with nondual spirituality could be a plus, but it wasn't a necessity. Nothing extra was necessary.

At that time I had no means of doing that, but the means quickly arrived as I wrote my first book, *The Book of Undoing*. It wasn't about information, it was about presentation. And that's what I've been doing ever since. Rational Awakening, which employs The Living Method to bring it about, is a remarkable singularity. Just to keep it from being too easy for Itself to tell Itself the truth, Oneness hid this vehicle inside of one of the most tarnished things It had lying about, and that's been wonderfully successful at slowing this thing down.

I refer here, of course, to this unit.

FRED DAVIS

FRED DAVIS studied and practiced Eastern wisdom for twenty-five years prior to 2006, when seeking ended, and his true awakening commenced. He is the creator and editor of Awakening Clarity Now, and the founder of *The Living Method of Awakening.*

Fred is also the author of three books:

The Book of Undoing:
Direct Pointing to Nondual Awareness,

The Book of Unknowing:
From Enlightenment to Embodiment,

Beyond Recovery:
Nonduality and the Twelve Steps.

The Living Method of Awakening is an extraordinarily successful process of inquiry, investigation, and direct pointing that encourages immediate recognition of our shared True Nature. Hundreds of people on six continents have found the door to freedom using The Living Method, which has roots in both Eastern spirituality and Western philosophy.

Made in the USA
San Bernardino, CA
23 November 2015